Favorite Hymns
Word Search

By the Same Author . . .

Bible Word Search Puzzles

Favorite Hymns Word Search

by
DIANE BRUMMEL BLOEM

ZONdERVAN PUBLISHING HOUSE
OF THE ZONDERVAN CORPORATION
GRAND RAPIDS, MICHIGAN 49506

FAVORITE HYMNS WORD SEARCH
Copyright © 1976 by The Zondervan Corporation
Grand Rapids, Michigan

Second printing   1977
ISBN 0-310-21352-5

Printed in the United States of America

*This book is lovingly dedicated
to my parents,
WILLIAM and MARY BRUMMEL,
who taught me to know the
Lord, and to love to sing
His praises.*

FOREWORD

When you think of your treasures, do you count among them the many hymns which help you voice your praise to God? The apostle Paul tells us to be filled with the Holy Spirit and to "speak to one another in the words of psalms, hymns, and sacred songs; sing hymns and psalms to the Lord, with praise in your hearts" (Ephesians 5:19, TEV). Paul practiced what he preached. He and Silas comforted one another with the singing of God's praises as they sat chained to prison walls in the dark of night.

Is prison in your future? Many believers, even today, are imprisoned for their faith. Will your eyesight last forever? Many sightless Christians give thanks for parents and teachers who urged them to memorize Scripture and songs. Do you always have a hymnbook nearby when praises to God well up in your heart? Your praise will find ready words wherever you are and whatever you may be doing if you can draw from the treasure house of your memory the words of precious songs of praise and supplication.

The purpose of this book is to encourage you and to aid you as you review and memorize hymns that have been favorites of believers for many years. You can test your memory as you draw from the word list and fill in the blanks in the text of the hymn. Then you can take each word on the list and find it hidden in the puzzle grid. Sing the words as you search and store up treasures of song.

The hidden words are all in a straight line, horizontal, vertical, or diagonal. They may be spelled forward or backward. Circle each word in the puzzle as you find it and underline it on the word list. Then, when all the words on the list are found, you may want to find other hidden words in the puzzle, just for fun, and make a list of all the extra words you find. Answers, if you need them, are found in the back of the book.

I pray that the words of these hymns may express the praise in your heart, as they express the praise in mine to the God who loved me and saved me and keeps me for time and for eternity.

Diane Bloem

Favorite Hymns Word Search

ALL HAIL THE POWER OF JESUS' NAME

All_____ the_____ of Jesus'_____!
Let_____ _____ fall;
Bring_____ the royal_____,
And_____ Him Lord of all!

Ye_____ _____ of Israel's race,
Ye_____ from the fall,
Hail Him who_____ you by His_____,
_____ crown_____ Lord of all!

Let every_____, _____ tribe,
_____ this_____ ball,
To Him all_____ _____,
And crown Him Lord_____ _____!

O that with_____ sacred_____
We at His_____ may_____!
We'll_____ the_____ song,
And crown Him_____ of all!

Edward Perronet – John Rippon

ALL HAIL THE POWER OF JESUS' NAME

- ALL
- AND
- ANGELS
- ASCRIBE
- CHOSEN
- CROWN
- DIADEM
- EVERLASTING
- EVERY
- FALL
- FEET
- FORTH
- GRACE
- HAIL
- HIM
- JOIN
- KINDRED
- LORD
- MAJESTY
- NAME
- ON
- OF
- POWER
- PROSTRATE
- RANSOMED
- SAVES
- SEED
- TERRESTRIAL
- THRONG
- YONDER

Terry L. Turner 6-11-84

AMAZING GRACE

Amazing grace! how sweet the sound,
That saved a wretch like me!
I once was lost, but now am found,
Was blind, but now I see.

'Twas grace that taught my heart to fear,
 and grace my fears relieved;
How precious did that grace appear
The hour I first believed!

Through many dangers, toils, and snares
I have already come;
'Tis grace hath brought me safe thus far,
And grace will lead me home.

When we've been there ten-thousand years,
Bright shining as the sun,
We've no less days to sing God's praise
Than when we first begun.

John Newton

AMAZING GRACE

```
L R E L I E V E D O R T H U S
A S U O I C E R P E D P S D T
K T T O H M N E T N A I T S H
S A V E D M U D A N G E R S O
W U M S A P G Y L E A I R I U
E G I A P P E A R V F I L N S
E H N G Z E B E E N O C W H A
T T O B L I N D A S U O E O N
F S T R H Y N T D O N P N N D
T H R O U G H G Y S D R A C E
T I H U O A S H U H L A T S E
T N H G R A C E O G I I S U O
S I O H L M E A T M K S E S E
Y N H T S N A R E S E E T K A
E G W H E N R T R L I N G C H
```

ALREADY ✓
AMAZING ✓
AND ✓
APPEAR ✓
BEEN ✓
BEGUN ✓
BLIND ✓
BROUGHT ✓
DANGERS ✓
FIRST ✓
FOUND ✓
GRACE ✓
HEART ✓
HOME
LESS ✓

LIKE ✓
NOW ✓
ONCE ✓
PRAISE ✓
PRECIOUS
RELIEVED ✗ (last word found)
SAVED ✓
SHINING ✓
SNARES ✓
SWEET ✓
TAUGHT ✓
THOUSAND ✓
THROUGH ✓
THUS ✓
WHEN ✓

A MIGHTY FORTRESS IS OUR GOD

A_____ _____is our_____,
A bulwark never_____;
Our_____He, amid the flood
Of_____ills_____.
For_____our_____foe
_____seek to work us_____;
His craft_____power are_____,
And,_____with_____hate,
On earth is not his_____.

Did_____in our_____
  strength_____,
Our_____would be losing,
_____not the_____Man on our side,
The Man of God's own_____.
_____ask who_____may be?
Christ Jesus, it is He;
Lord_____His name,
From_____to age the_____,
And He_____win the_____.

Martin Luther

A MIGHTY FORTRESS IS OUR GOD

```
G M U S T E Q U A E H T K I S
R O W N H J B L S S T I L L W
I E D G A F V A S S G F R F M
G M N D T I B E T N N A Y A G
H A H C P A R R I C I I T N O
T S R X O T I L C O S L H C Q
D S D T R V I B T N O I G I U
P F H O I A A W C F O N I E O
E Y F N V J H V B I H G M N G
K I G E K L T M Z D C O R T B
U L R R Q Z P A N E R E D A D
X P E T E U Y J V T P E T O E
W A E U S A A L A L M T T R W
M S N G R O T L E R L H E O E
R X N D A C D H A E O W E W Q
```

AGE	HELPER
ANCIENT	MIGHTY
AND	MORTAL
ARMED	MUST
BATTLE	OWN
CHOOSING	PREVAILING
CONFIDE	RIGHT
CRUEL	SABAOTH
DOST	SAME
DOTH	STILL
EQUAL	STRIVING
FAILING	THAT
FORTRESS	WE
GOD	WERE
GREAT	WOE

BENEATH THE CROSS OF JESUS

_____the cross of Jesus
I fain_____take my_____,
The shadow of a_____Rock
_____a_____land;
A home within the_____,
A_____upon the way,
_____the burning of the_____heat
And the_____of the day.

Upon that_____of Jesus
Mine eye at_____can_____
The very_____form of One
Who_____there for me;
And from my_____heart with tears
Two_____I confess —
The wonders of_____love
And my_____.

I_____, O cross, thy_____
For my_____place;
I ask no other_____than
The sunshine of His_____;
_____to let the world go by,
To know no_____nor loss,
My_____self my only_____,
My_____all the cross.

Elizabeth C. Clephane

BENEATH THE CROSS OF JESUS

```
S H A D O W T I O E K A T L E
Y C O N T E N T O A W I D E S
T R S U F F E R E D U L C O T
E O S M I T T E N N R A O S A
N S E I W E A R Y I F E H A N
D S N G S E M I T H W N T F D
H E R H S H A M E T O I A R T
E E E T G N I Y D I N H E O B
A S D Y W O U L D W D S N M B
P G L O R Y R E S T E N E E Y
H S I N F U L N E D R U B L G
U N W O R T H I N E S S A E A
W F O T N G N I D I B A Z T I
R H T R C E D I T N O O N A N
T A E I E G N I M E E D E R L
```

ABIDING	SHADOW
BENEATH	SHAME
BURDEN	SINFUL
CONTENT	SMITTEN
CROSS	STAND
DYING	SUFFERED
FACE	SUNSHINE
FROM	TAKE
GAIN	TIMES
GLORY	UNWORTHINESS
MIGHTY	WEARY
NOONTIDE	WILDERNESS
REDEEMING	WITHIN
REST	WONDERS
SEE	WOULD

BLESSED ASSURANCE

Blessed _Assurance_, Jesus is mine!
Oh, what a _foretaste_ of glory divine!
Heir of _Salvation_, purchase of God,
Born of His Spirit, _washed_ in His blood.

CHORUS:
This is my _story_, this is my song,
Praising my Saviour _all_ the day long;
This is my story, this is my _song_,
Praising my _Savior_ all the day _long_.

Perfect _submission_, _perfect_ delight,
Visions of rapture now burst on my _sight_:
Angels _descending_ bring from above
Echoes of mercy, _whispers_ of love.

Perfect submission, all is at _rest_,
I in my Savior am _happy_ and blest;
Watching and _waiting_, looking above,
Filled with His _goodness_, lost in His love.

Fanny J. Crosby

BLESSED ASSURANCE

```
F O R E T A S T E I S A R D M
G S L S T O R Y A N T U H E A
P A U I T N D E O D O W C S T
E L D B G U O I T I T N O C N
R V I G M O S H V T A D L E O
F A N W T I G A I R V L E N M
E T S A V U S O U O A M T D E
C I R S C P H S W I H G S I K
T O E H W R S O I N N Y L N E
T N P E H A E K I O D O S G A
Y W S D N I D A S E N R H E R
P C I E O S U G L G D R E S T
P O H U O I W A I T I N G T B
A T W U N N O S S E N D O O G
H O M S I G H T W T N O E W W
```

July 7th 1984
Terry L. Turner

ALL
ASSURANCE
DESCENDING
FORETASTE
GOODNESS
HAPPY
LONG
PERFECT
PRAISING
REST

SALVATION
SAVIOUR
SIGHT
SONG
STORY
SUBMISSION
VISIONS
WAITING
WASHED
WHISPERS

BRING THEM IN

Hark! 'tis the_____voice I hear,
Out in the_____dark and_____,
Calling the sheep who've gone_____
_____from the Shepherd's fold away.

Chorus:

Bring_____in, bring them in,
_____them in from the fields of_____;
Bring them_____, bring them in,
Bring the_____ones to Jesus.

Who'll go and help this Shepherd_____,
Help Him the wandering_____to find?
Who'll bring the lost ones to the_____
Where they'll be_____from the cold?

_____in the desert hear their _____,
Out on the_____wild and high;
_____! 'tis the Master_____to thee,
"Go find my_____wher-e'er they be."

Alexcenah Thomas

BRING THEM IN

```
D E C R Y B M H E B F O G P S
C E W B X I O G C R N H M I Q
S K S V C J Z D P I X I N L K
H J U E D O T F R N I E K F I
E L M T R N A W N G R S W D N
P M S P E T S P O A U S H J D
H O H K A B N E Z I Q P Z C I
E U E O R C S H E L T E R E D
R N E Z E J K X A C D A Q B C
D T P H O M Y S V R B K E X T
S A G J A P T E Q O U S A F H
E I S T J R A R C U P Y G J E
N N A H A M K U A T R F A R M
O S V Y B U Q L T M J O R Y Z
T F O L D N W A N D E R I N G
```

ASTRAY	MOUNTAINS
BRING	ONES
CRY	OUT
DESERT	SHEEP
DREAR	SHELTERED
FAR	SHEPHERD'S
FOLD	SIN
HARK	SPEAKS
IN	THEM
KIND	WANDERING

COME, THOU ALMIGHTY KING

Come, Thou_____King,
Help us Thy name to_____,
_____us to praise:
Father, all glorious,
O'er all_____,
Come and_____over us,
_____of Days.

Come, Thou_____Word,
_____on Thy_____sword,
Our_____attend:
_____, and Thy_____bless,
And_____Thy word_____:
Spirit of_____,
On us_____.

Come, Holy_____,
Thy sacred_____bear
In this glad_____:
_____who almighty art,
Now_____in every heart,
And ne'er from us_____,
_____of power.

To the_____One in Three
_____praises be,
Hence_____:
His_____majesty
May we in_____see,
And to_____
_____and adore.

Author Unknown

COME, THOU ALMIGHTY KING

```
E T E R N A L A S X T B D Y P
H D R M I G H T Y N V R A C R
E U W A E Z S S E N I L O H A
L G S T P E V I G G E R F P Y
P M A O H E C O M E L E I R E
M O L L V N D I K Q P T R J R
H N M N A E V E R M O R E O L
O P I N C A R N A T E O I Q G
U R G E S T A E R G P F G E T
R T H O U T I R I P S M N L G
U F T D V Y R O L G W O X U N
Y C Y T I N R E T E N C Z R I
D E S C E N D A W I T N E S S
E K L O V E I A S S E C C U S
B O J U H S U O I R O T C I V
```

ALMIGHTY	HOUR
ANCIENT	INCARNATE
COME	LOVE
COMFORTER	MIGHTY
DEPART	PEOPLE
DESCEND	PRAYER
ETERNAL	REIGN
ETERNITY	RULE
EVERMORE	SING
GIRD	SOVEREIGN
GIVE	SPIRIT
GLORY	SUCCESS
GREAT	THOU
HELP	VICTORIOUS
HOLINESS	WITNESS

COME, THOU FOUNT

Come, Thou _____ of every _____,
_____ my _____ to sing Thy grace;
_____ of _____, never ceasing,
Call for _____ of loudest _____.
Teach me some _____ sonnet,
Sung by _____ _____ above;
Praise the _____ — I'm fixed upon it —
Mount of Thy redeeming _____.

Here I raise mine _____;
_____ by Thy help I'm come;
And I hope, by Thy good _____,
_____ to arrive at _____.
Jesus _____ me when a stranger,
_____ from the fold of God;
He, to rescue me from danger,
_____ His precious blood.

O to _____ how _____ a debtor
Daily I'm _____ to be!
Let Thy _____, like a _____,
Bind my wandering heart to Thee:
_____ to wander, Lord, I feel it,
Prone to _____ the God I love;
Here's my heart, O take and seal it;
_____ it for Thy _____ above.

Robert Robinson

COME, THOU FOUNT

```
M E L O D I O U S E S I A R P
P S V E Z M Y Q N W E V O L L
R L F L A M I N G X M T A K E
P R O N E V U T N U O M J O A
D I B T R A E H I T H E R L S
F E T T E R T E N U T S A R U
N O S O U G H T G P H E Q G R
T N U O F G A N E R S I O N E
A K S B P L I Y C R E M C I M
G U K S T R E A M S Z A F S S
R H A A E B E N E Z E R T S G
A U G D O V S T R U O C E E N
C O N S T R A I N E D B D L O
E A T O N G U E S I F W C B S
W E Y L E F A S S E N D O O G
```

BLESSING
CONSTRAINED
COURTS
EBENEZER
FETTER
FLAMING
FOUNT
GOODNESS
GRACE
GREAT
HEART
HITHER
HOME
INTERPOSED
LEAVE

LOVE
MELODIOUS
MERCY
MOUNT
PLEASURE
PRAISE
PRONE
SAFELY
SEAL
SONGS
SOUGHT
STREAMS
TONGUES
TUNE
WANDERING

COUNT YOUR BLESSINGS

When upon life's_____ you are tempest tossed,
When you are_____, thinking all is lost,
_____ your many blessings, name them one by one,
And it will_____ you what the Lord hath done.

Chorus:

Count your_____,
_____ them one by one;
Count_____ blessings,
_____ what God hath done;
Count your blessings,
Name_____ one by one;
Count your_____ blessings,
See what God_____ done.

Are you_____ burdened with a_____ of care?
Does the_____ seem heavy you are called to_____?
Count your many blessings, every_____ will fly,
_____ you will be_____ as the days go by.

When you_____ at others with their _____ and gold,
Think that Christ has_____ you His wealth _____;
Count your many blessings, _____ cannot buy
Your_____ in heaven, nor your home on_____.

So, amid the_____, whether great or small,
Do not be discouraged, _____ is over all;
Count your many blessings,_____ will attend,
Help and_____ give you to your_____ end.

Johnson Oatman, Jr.

COUNT YOUR BLESSINGS

```
C O M F O R T A L O O K S B P
O O C E G O D D H I D F I G R
N J U L O M P R D L O T N U O
F N Q N K E M A N S E E G R M
L O A D T S T W U A H G I H I
I V X A N D W E Y N Z A N E S
C D I S C O U R A G E D G Z E
T I O S G N I S S E L B U A D
J O U R N E Y S U L T W B O C
Y U R H T A H T R S B H U I U
S C R O S S S I P W R B E M H
R Z D M A D E A R G T H M M Y
A E Y N N M V A I Y O U R E N
E A R A E O L B S R E V E L A
B I L L O W S M E D Y E N O M
```

AND	JOURNEY'S
ANGELS	LANDS
BEAR	LOAD
BILLOWS	LOOK
BLESSINGS	MANY
COMFORT	MONEY
CONFLICT	NAME
COUNT	PROMISED
CROSS	REWARD
DISCOURAGED	SEE
DOUBT	SINGING
EVER	SURPRISE
GOD	THEM
HATH	UNTOLD
HIGH	YOUR

DAY IS DYING IN THE WEST

Day is_____in the_____,
_____is touching_____with rest;
Wait and_____while the_____
_____her_____lamps alight
_____all_____sky.

_____of life,_____the dome
Of the_____, Thy_____,
Gather us, who_____Thy face
To the fold of Thy_____,
For_____art nigh.

When_____from_____sight
_____the_____, the day, the_____,
Lord of_____, on our_____
_____eternal_____rise,
And_____end.

Refrain:
Holy, Holy, _____, Lord God of Hosts!
Heaven and earth are_____of Thee!
Heaven and earth are praising Thee,
O Lord_____high!

Mary A. Lathbury

DAY IS DYING IN THE WEST

```
C W O R S H I P D I A E B D F
G T E S L E G N A H C B N I E
K H B J F G N I N E V E L T M
N R S S A P I A O X V N S P W
Q O Y R A R N S S A T E Y E S
W U N I V E R S E V W A H U E
A G I X Z V O H Y T O T U Z E
I H G O J E M A S U S H A C A
B W H C H R F D T G V I A V R
K X T D I O E O A G J R H N T
H E Y O A F E W R I B U R U H
U O M A D L U S S M T U M B U
P O L O R D K L E T O S R O C
E Q H Y H R Z S L E Q S H T P
D Y I N G L F M G N K T T O I
```

ANGELS	MOST
BENEATH	NIGHT
DYING	OUR
EARTH	PASS
EMBRACE	SEEK
EVENING	SETS
EYES	SHADOWS
FOREVER	STARS
FULL	THE
HEAVEN	THOU
HOLY	THROUGH
HOME	UNIVERSE
LET	WEST
LORD	WORSHIP
MORNING	

DOES JESUS CARE?

Does_____care when my_____is pained
Too_____for mirth and song;
As the_____press, and the cares_____,
And the_____grows_____and long?

Chorus:

O yes, He_____ — I know He cares,
His heart is_____with my grief;
When the_____are weary, the long
    nights_____,
I know my_____cares.

Does Jesus care when my way is_____
With a_____dread and fear?
As the_____fades into_____night
    shades,
Does He care_____to be_____?

_____Jesus care when I've_____and
    failed
To resist some_____strong;
When for my deep_____I find no relief,
_____my tears_____all the
    night_____?

Does Jesus care when I've said good-by
To the_____on earth to me,
And my_____heart_____till it
    _____breaks —
Is it_____to Him? Does He see?

Frank E. Graeff

DOES JESUS CARE?

```
H I T T D E H C U O T I G O I
E S D E E P L Y T S E R A E D
A N E M B S L I T N M N I T H
R E E R I R N E Y A P T H E E
T D O S A S O R R C T K R A D
F R S E H C A J S S A I S F A
E U N A M E L E S S T A Y R Y
I B N U R N W S O A I U A J L
P E E D T O D A L V O E D E I
G A K E M U H D L I N Y S S G
R T D A U G H T N O A T W U H
I H W E U H S H S U N R A S T
E H I O M F E A O R W G Y D O
F T H G L O O W E A R Y I A N
Y T R K C F D I S T R E S S W
```

ACHES	GRIEF
AUGHT	HEART
BURDENS	JESUS
CARES	LONG
DARK	NAMELESS
DAYLIGHT	NEAR
DAYS	NEARLY
DEAREST	SAD
DEEP	SAVIOUR
DEEPLY	TEMPTATION
DISTRESS	THOUGH
DOES	TOUCHED
DREARY	TRIED
ENOUGH	WAY
FLOW	WEARY

FAITH OF OUR FATHERS

Faith of our_____! living_____
In spite of_____, fire, and sword —
O how our_____beat high with_____
When-e'er we hear that_____word!
Faith of our fathers, holy faith!
We will be_____to thee till death!

Our fathers, chained in_____dark,
Were still in heart and_____free;
How sweet would be their_____fate,
If_____, like them, could_____for thee!
Faith of our fathers, holy faith!
We will be true to thee till death!

_____of our fathers! we will_____
Both_____and foe in all our_____,
And_____thee, too, as love_____how,
By_____words and_____life:
Faith of our fathers, holy faith!
We will be true to thee till death!

Frederick W. Faber

FAITH OF OUR FATHERS

```
G L O R I O U S T O L N T G I
Y A K E C I N A J L E Y H B H
T C S E M A J H I E L L O V E
J O Y M E A A T D C A D K E A
I N T S N O S I R P W N A S R
A S N U Y T T E B A O I N G T
L C R O E E B M O E F K L E S
C I O U A I K E G I M E O L B
D E T T D I D N E I R F S S I
R N N R T H U A E O V A T E N
A C H I L D R E N S R T R U E
N E I V G T N F A I T H I O B
O H S W O N K T H E Y E F W A
E P R E A C H K I Y A R E G E
L N R H D R A H C I R S F R O
```

CHILDREN'S
CONSCIENCE
DIE
DUNGEON
FAITH
FATHERS
FRIEND
GLORIOUS
HEARTS
JOY

KINDLY
KNOWS
LOVE
PREACH
PRISONS
STILL
STRIFE
THEY
TRUE
VIRTUOUS

GOD BE WITH YOU

God be with you till we meet again;
By His_____guide, _____you,
With His sheep_____fold_____;
God be with you till we meet again.

God be with you till we meet again;
'Neath_____wings_____hide you,
Daily_____still_____you;
God be with you till we meet again.

God be with you till we meet again;
When_____perils thick_____you,
Put His arms_____round you;
God be with you till we meet again.

God be_____you till we meet again;
_____love's_____floating o'er you,
Smite death's_____wave_____you;
God be with you till we meet again.

Chorus:

Till we_____, till we meet,
_____we meet at Jesus' feet;
Till we meet, till we meet,
_____be with you till we meet_____.

Jeremiah E. Rankin

GOD BE WITH YOU

```
S F C H D P C E I R E N N A B
E H M A N F R O I G O J I K P
C M E E T B L O U M A N N A M
U N G G O Q C E V N P J T Q U
R V R N N S B T H I S D U Z A
E V L I W I K P P X D E Y R U
L Z A L E N N E R E B E L C P
Y I D I I E S E O X F O G S H
H I U A A J B K T K G O D L O
W M G F T I L L E A C N D Y L
O A E N P W E Q C H E R Y O D
S F T U G I U H T I W R V U J
B E F O R E W L I F E S H K X
Y A L M N Q Z T N R E U I T O
C O N F O U N D G U A O S P B
```

AGAIN	MEET
BANNER	PROTECTING
BEFORE	PROVIDE
CONFOUND	SECURELY
COUNSELS	THREATENING
GOD	TILL
HIS	UNFAILING
KEEP	UPHOLD
LIFE'S	WITH
MANNA	YOU

HARK! THE HERALD ANGELS SING

Hark! the _____ angels _____,
"Glory to the _____ King;
_____ on earth, and mercy _____ —
God and _____ reconciled!"
Joyful, all ye _____, rise,
Join the triumph of the _____;
With the _____ hosts proclaim,
"Christ is born in _____!"

_____, by _____ heaven adored,
Christ, the Everlasting _____!
Late in time _____ Him come,
_____ of a Virgin's _____:
Veiled in flesh the _____ see;
Hail the _____ Deity!
_____ as man with _____ to dwell,
Jesus, our _____.

_____ the heaven-born _____ of Peace!
Hail the Sun of _____!
Light and life to all He _____;
Risen with _____ in His wings.
Mild He lays His _____ by,
Born that man no more may die,
Born to raise the sons of _____,
Born to give them _____ birth.

_____! the herald angels sing,
"Glory to the newborn King!"

Charles Wesley

HARK! THE HERALD ANGELS SING

```
A I P L E A S E D H A R K C A
M N A T I O N S B N Q D O N P
T C U M E H E L H T E B G R S
G A G I E Y M B E X F E W V G
N R Z L M N M R K L L H J P O
I N N D H O A I I I W O M B D
L A G S N J N N C Q F L S H H
A T L E E T U G K F R D S A E
E E O C W C E S S U L I I I A
H V R A B H L P L O R D N L D
S G Y E O R R H T R A E N G H
E F Y P R I N C E X E I E N W
I C Z A N S D L A R E H R I D
K R I G H T E O U S N E S S E
S E C O N D B H I G H E S T A
```

ANGELIC
BEHOLD
BETHLEHEM
BRINGS
CHRIST
EARTH
EMMANUEL
GLORY
GODHEAD
HAIL
HARK
HEALING
HERALD
HIGHEST
INCARNATE
LORD
MEN
MILD
NATIONS
NEWBORN
OFFSPRING
PEACE
PLEASED
PRINCE
RIGHTEOUSNESS
SECOND
SING
SINNERS
SKIES
WOMB

HOLY, HOLY, HOLY!

Holy, _Holy_, Holy! Lord God _Almighty_!
Early in the _morning_ our
   song shall _rise_ to Thee;
Holy, Holy, Holy! _Merciful_ and Mighty!
God in Three _Persons_, blessed Trinity!

Holy, Holy, Holy! All the _saints_ adore Thee,
Casting down their golden _crowns_ around
   the _glassy_ sea;
Cherubim and _Seraphim_ falling _down_ before
   Thee,
Which _wert_ and art and evermore
   shall be.

Holy, Holy, Holy! Tho' the _____ hide Thee,
Tho' the _eye_ of sinful _man_ Thy glory
   may not see;
Only Thou art holy; there is none
   beside Thee
Perfect in _power_, in love, and _purity_.

Holy, Holy, Holy! _Lord_ God Almighty!
All Thy _____ shall praise Thy name, in
   earth, and sky, and _sea_;
Holy, Holy, Holy! Merciful and _mighty_!
God in _three_ Persons, blessed _Trinity_!

Reginald Heber

HOLY, HOLY, HOLY!

```
E Y E L P N A M O S A S B H R
W Z T M R E W O P L S Q O T W
A E C I D N D G M E G L L O F
H V R I N J N I N L Y A R E N
K I S T S I G K M P H K N Q W
U E R O T H R E E S S X O S O
B S N S T A Y T M I G H T Y D
T G A Y D T U I E O J Y H Y Y
E C K I I O H I R A R N L W S
A G M R N P W L C P R N V O S
R Q U X A T R N I R O L I S A
T P Y R T A S U F B O E Y N L
H Z E Y L O R D U Z C W A F G
X S N O S R E P L D G E N E H
A R I S E V L C J M S D N S F
```

7-2-84
July Terry L. Turner

ALMIGHTY
BESIDE
CASTING
CROWNS
DARKNESS
DOWN
EARLY
EARTH
EYE
GLASSY
HOLY
LORD
MAN
MERCIFUL
MIGHTY

MORNING
ONLY
PERSONS
POWER
PURITY
RISE
SAINTS
SEA
SERAPHIM
SHALT
SONG
THREE
TRINITY
WERT
WORKS

I KNOW WHOM I HAVE BELIEVED

I know not why God's_____grace
To me He hath made_____,
Nor why, _____, Christ in love
_____me for His own.

Chorus:

But "I know whom I have believed,
 and am_____
that He is_____
To keep that which I've_____
Unto Him_____that day."

I know not how this_____faith
To me He did_____,
Nor how_____in His Word
_____peace within my heart.

I know not how the Spirit_____,
_____men of sin,
Revealing Jesus_____the Word,
_____faith in Him.

I know not when my Lord may_____,
At night or_____fair,
Nor if I'll walk the_____with Him,
Or_____Him in the air.

Daniel W. Whittle

I KNOW WHOM I HAVE BELIEVED

```
I T H R O U G H T A M N A V G
E N G N I V E I L E B O A D A
B E N I I S N C G A U L D M G
G N I T A E R C I B E S E I A
N I C O M E M I Y D U T T L I
O K N O W N A S E L E R T E N
R T I H I Y A D N O O N I M S
S L V E Y B A A T B G N M M T
I U N E P U H E A S N T M U W
M B O R S O E Z A E T L O R A
P E C R T M C V O V R N C B E
A L E R D P I W R O U G H T W
R P I T E N Y R T M I E R S A
T S L A G W O D E M E E D E R
U D N A I U N W O R T H Y E L
```

ABLE	MOVES
AGAINST	NOONDAY
BELIEVING	PERSUADED
COME	REDEEMED
COMMITTED	SAVING
CONVINCING	THROUGH
CREATING	UNWORTHY
IMPART	VALE
KNOWN	WONDROUS
MEET	WROUGHT

I LOVE TO TELL THE STORY

I_____to tell the_____of_____things above,
Of Jesus and His glory, of_____and His love.
I love to tell the story,_____I know 'tis true;
It_____my longing as_____else can do.

Chorus:

I love to tell the story,
'Twill be my_____in glory
To tell the old, old story
Of Jesus and His love.

I love to tell the story, more wonderful it_____
Than all the golden_____of all our
_____dreams.
I love to tell the story, it did so much for me;
And that is just the_____I tell it now to thee.

I love to tell the story, 'tis_____to repeat
What seems, each time I tell it, more _____sweet.
I love to tell the story, for some have never
_____
The message of_____from God's own Holy Word.

I love to tell the story, for those who_____it best
Seem_____and thirsting to hear it like the rest.
And when, in_____of glory, I sing the new, new song,
'Twill be the old, old story that I have loved so
_____.

Katherine Hankey

I LOVE TO TELL THE STORY

```
O N E O R D N I S C E N E S E
R A N E H E A R D O C U S T L
O T E H D S N R E I M E S A C
W W R L P O B E C A U S E T R
T O O V O E V O L K J E S U S
S G N N O T H I N G U I U E T
A T O G D O O D N L W F N O H
P N S M E E S I S O K S S R E
K N O W O T R F O N R I E A M
Y R O T S E K F A G S T E M E
T G N I G H E O U O R A N R W
N A E N O I T A V L A S S U S
G N U F A N C I E S L L M U B
T H O G E N O S A E R Y T B H
P L E A S A N T N R O H R O K
```

BECAUSE	PLEASANT
FANCIES	REASON
GOLDEN	SALVATION
HEARD	SATISFIES
HUNGERING	SCENES
JESUS	SEEMS
KNOW	STORY
LONG	THEME
LOVE	UNSEEN
NOTHING	WONDERFULLY

IN MY HEART THERE RINGS A MELODY

I_____a song that_____gave me,
It was sent from_____above;
There_____was a sweeter_____,
'Tis a melody of_____.

Chorus:

In my_____there rings a melody,
There_____a melody with heaven's
 _____;
In my heart there rings a melody;
There rings a melody of love.

I love the Christ who died on_____,
For He_____my sins_____;
He put_____my heart a melody,
And I_____it's_____to stay.

'Twill be my_____theme in glory,
_____the angels I will_____;
'Twill be a song with_____harmony,
When the_____of heaven ring.

Elton M. Roth

IN MY HEART THERE RINGS A MELODY

```
H E A V E N O P S E V A H E O
A W A Y W R D S I N O Y E I T
R T H R E D I V A D Y R A R R
M Y N A E N N E K L O A R O E
O H I V T H G C N E J M T L B
N T G L O R I O U S U S E J O
Y A R A P U T U T S I K C I R
E K D C I S A R O D K N O W Y
S T H P L A R T H E R E P O R
A T L D C W A S H E D V H L A
L E U O R I N G S W U E I E M
G I H I N T S K Y E O R L S E
U R W I T H I N O V Z W I S S
O A K C A J N E H O T M P U O
D H T O T R G M E L O D Y R R
```

AWAY	KNOW
CALVARY	LOVE
COURTS	MELODY
ENDLESS	NEVER
GLORIOUS	RINGS
HARMONY	SING
HAVE	THERE
HEART	WASHED
HEAVEN	WITH
JESUS	WITHIN

IN THE GARDEN

I come to the _garden_ alone,
while the dew is _fresh_ on the roses,
And the _sound_ I hear,
falling on my ear,
The Son of God _calling_.

Chorus:
And He _walks_ with me, _and_ He talks with me,
And He _tells_ me I am His own,
And the joy we share as we _tarry_ there,
None _other_ has ever _known_.

He_____, and the sound of His voice
Is so_____ the birds hush their_____,
And the_____
That He gave to me,
_____ my heart is ringing.

I'd_____ in the garden with Him
Though the night around me be falling,
But He bids me go;
_____ the voice of woe,
His voice to me is_____.

C. Austin Miles

IN THE GARDEN

I Love you

```
A N D L O E B D I A N E E S T
H W I T H I N E L J O B Y W B
L Y C A L L I N G M O E M E M
S A R W H I L E X Y C D E E O
I B D L D I S C L O S E S T O
N V E M S W A L K S W I L Z L
G I S A P M F A L L I N G B R
I U T E E M M V O I C E F E G
N L A M A U R Y G A R D E N V
G O Y S K S B R T H R O U G H
H U M L S I M J E N W O N K K
L K A I T E R I S L L E T E O
M L E I M R Y D O L E M S N M
P A B T Q L Y R R A T O R E S
M D I S R R E H T O K B L O T
```

- ~~AND~~
- ~~CALLING~~
- ~~DISCLOSES~~
- ~~FALLING~~
- ~~GARDEN~~
- ~~KNOWN~~
- ~~MELODY~~
- ~~OTHER~~
- ~~SINGING~~
- ~~SPEAKS~~
- ~~STAY~~
- ~~STILL~~
- ~~SWEET~~
- ~~TARRY~~
- ~~TELLS~~
- ~~THROUGH~~
- ~~VOICE~~
- ~~WALKS~~
- ~~WHILE~~
- ~~WITHIN~~

Terry L.

Twem
8-6-84

I THINK WHEN I READ THAT SWEET STORY

I_____when I_____that sweet _____of old,
When Jesus was here_____men,
How He called little_____as lambs to His _____,
I_____like to have_____with Him then.

I_____that His hands had been_____on my head,
That His arms had been thrown_____me,
And that I_____have seen His kind look when He_____,
"Let the_____ones come unto Me."

Yet still to His_____in prayer I may go,
And_____for a share in_____love;
And if I thus_____seek Him below,
I_____see Him and hear Him_____.

Jemima Thompson Luke

I THINK WHEN I READ THAT SWEET STORY

```
A Y E R F F E J W I S H W K N
H M E N A B O V E J A M E S W
T D O H E E R O D N U O R A A
L L L N I E S S I N N E D S D
C A L U G N D I V A D E A O M
N E E R O D H I S Y C N U A C
L L E D N H O J U A D G R H P
O E A R N E S T L Y L Y I O K
O H E N R Y N P D A A L E R N
T F O L D S I L S N D A V E I
S L E L T T I L N R E A D B H
T S A I D E T H E I K C I V T
O E L L A H S N R E T H G I M
O S T O R Y I N A J Y H T A K
F K I M B E R L Y H T O R O D
```

ABOVE
AMONG
AROUND
ASK
BEEN
CHILDREN
EARNESTLY
FOLD
FOOTSTOOL
HIS

LITTLE
MIGHT
PLACED
READ
SAID
SHALL
SHOULD
STORY
THINK
WISH

JESUS, LOVER OF MY SOUL

Jesus, _____ of my soul,
Let me to Thy _____ fly,
_____ the _____ waters roll,
While the _____ still is high.
Hide me, O my _____, hide,
Till the _____ of life is _____;
Safe into the _____ guide,
O _____ my soul at last!

Other _____ have I none;
Hangs my helpless _____ on Thee;
_____, ah, leave me not alone,
Still _____ and comfort me.
All my trust on Thee is _____,
All my _____ from Thee I bring;
Cover my _____ head
With the shadow of Thy _____.

Thou, O Christ, art all I _____;
More than all in Thee I find;
_____ the fallen, cheer the faint,
Heal the _____, and lead the blind.
Just and _____ is Thy name,
I am all _____;
False and full of sin I am,
_____ art full of truth and grace.

_____ grace with Thee is found,
Grace to _____ all my sin;
Let the healing streams _____;
Make and keep me _____ within.
Thou of life the _____ art,
Freely let me take of Thee;
Spring Thou up within my heart,
Rise to all _____.

Charles Wesley

JESUS, LOVER OF MY SOUL

```
H T O E F O U N T A I N N P O
Y M A I L L I W R U O I V A S
S S E N S U O E T H G I R N U
U S A B O U N D R M T F A O L
O O E M O S O B R I O D I R K
E U B L O E M O A Y R E S A B
T L C R E D T H E L P E E E E
N F I E T S U P P O R T S V L
E J R V E K N R L H M N I A I
L U G O R T W E O U P E C E H
P S H C N N I V F Q C R K L W
T H O U I A N O T E M P E S T
T P A S T W G L R V D W X Y Z
A S T A Y E D B C R E R A E N
N E V A H W A N T R E F U G E
```

ABOUND
BOSOM
COVER
DEFENSELESS
ETERNITY
FOUNTAIN
HAVEN
HELP
HOLY
LEAVE
LOVER
NEARER
PAST
PLENTEOUS
PURE

RAISE
RECEIVE
REFUGE
SAVIOUR
SICK
SOUL
STAYED
STORM
SUPPORT
TEMPEST
THOU
UNRIGHTEOUSNESS
WANT
WHILE
WING

JESUS LOVES ME

_____loves me! this I_____,
For the_____tells me so;
_____ones to Him belong;
They are weak, but He is_____.

Chorus:
Yes, Jesus_____me,
_____, Jesus loves me,
Yes, Jesus loves_____ —
The Bible_____me so.

Jesus loves me! He who_____,
_____gate to open wide;
He will_____away my sin,
Let His little_____come in.

Jesus loves me! loves me_____,
Though I'm very weak and ill;
From His_____throne on high,
Comes to_____me where I lie.

Jesus loves me! He will_____
Close_____me all the way;
If I love Him, _____I die
He will take me_____on high.

Anna B. Warner

JESUS LOVES ME

```
A D O H R H T U R E N E L R A
I S H I N I N G N S A M O H T
M T E L L S W A T C H Y H E A
R R A W A S H L E A H C I M L
L O V E S T I L L T K C A J L
T N E M E A C H I L D Y A K E
H G N H E Y E S T A L L I R N
T R S H T U R S T I L L E R U
E J E S U S I N L K G D S A S
N G I A R C W H E N B I B L E
N M A R D N A S H O M E E L Y
E I N A H P E T S W O D D Y R
K F Y L L A S B E S I D E A A
I T H N A S U S A S S I L E M
O L E A H C I M E S I N E D F
```

BESIDE	ME
BIBLE	SHINING
CHILD	STAY
DIED	STILL
HEAVEN'S	STRONG
HOME	TELLS
JESUS	WASH
KNOW	WATCH
LITTLE	WHEN
LOVES	YES

JESUS SAVES!

We have_____the joyful_____:
_____saves! Jesus_____!
Spread the_____all around:
Jesus saves! Jesus saves!
_____the news to every_____,
Climb the_____and cross the_____;
Onward! 'tis_____Lord's command;
Jesus saves! Jesus saves!

Waft it on the_____tide:
Jesus saves! Jesus saves!
Tell to_____far and_____:
Jesus saves! Jesus saves!
Sing, ye_____of the sea;
Echo back, ye_____caves;
Earth shall keep her_____:
Jesus saves! Jesus saves!

_____above the_____strife:
Jesus saves! Jesus saves!
By His_____and endless_____,
Jesus saves! Jesus saves!
Sing it_____through the gloom,
When the heart for_____craves;
Sing in triumph o'er the_____ —
Jesus saves! Jesus saves!

_____the winds a_____voice,
Jesus saves! Jesus saves!
Let the nations now_____,
Jesus saves! Jesus saves!
Shout_____full and free,
_____hills and_____caves;
This our song of_____ —
Jesus saves! Jesus saves!

Priscilla J. Owens

JESUS SAVES!

```
J U B I L E E S T S E P E E D
S T N I E V I G O E L A N D M
A D O G H N T W S F E T E H I
V N W A N E O V I C T O R Y G
E U H E A R D I O W T L L O H
S O R J E S U S T N A S Y U T
E S L E E D I W T A N V O R Y
S V T I D I N G S I V S E I O
I T S E I Y C R E M I L T S N
N H T A E D B H U R T S A D B
G N A T H P G E I T N Y A S M
D S D N A L S I A M N A E C O
R T E H G T S B U R M Y R A T
H I G H E S T P E C I O J E R
J R O L L I N G S L I F E O N
```

BATTLE	OUR
BEAR	REJOICE
DEATH	ROLLING
DEEPEST	SALVATION
GIVE	SAVES
HEARD	SING
HIGHEST	SINNERS
ISLANDS	SOFTLY
JESUS	SOUND
JUBILEE	STEEPS
LAND	TIDINGS
LIFE	TOMB
MERCY	VICTORY
MIGHTY	WAVES
OCEAN	WIDE

JOY TO THE WORLD!

Joy_____the_____! the_____is come;
Let_____receive her_____;
Let_____heart prepare_____room,
And_____and nature sing.

Joy to_____earth! the_____reigns;
Let_____their_____employ;
_____fields and_____, rocks,
_____and plains
Repeat the_____joy.

No_____let sins and_____grow,
_____thorns_____the ground;
He comes to make His_____flow
Far as the_____is found.

He_____the world with truth and_____,
_____makes the_____prove
The glories_____His_____,
And_____of His_____.

Issac Watts

JOY TO THE WORLD!

```
J O R U L E S A N O T P D S S
T L M L R B Q S W O R R O S A
Y U O L B F L O O D S C S N V
V R W V E A I E F K Z E F O I
D M E C E X T D S E N E T I O
I O B V H S G O J S G K H T R
A R U L E I U N U U I Y E A S
M E O F H N O O S E E N U N O
K P N O D I E R D V A S G W N
N I E I Q T R S T N X R R S G
A Z N W H I L E Y A A E T U S
Q G S G T L U V W C X Y Z H C
R P I O I N L H E A V E N M K
G R I H F J H I S R E D N O W
E D W O R L D M C M E N B F A
```

AND
BLESSINGS
CURSE
EARTH
EVERY
FLOODS
GRACE
HEAVEN
HILLS
HIM
INFEST
KING
LORD
LOVE
MEN
MORE
NATIONS
NOR
OF
RIGHTEOUSNESS
RULES
SAVIOR
SONGS
SORROWS
SOUNDING
THE
TO
WHILE
WONDERS
WORLD

MY COUNTRY, 'TIS OF THEE

My_____, 'tis of_____,
Sweet land of_____,
Of thee I_____:
_____where my fathers_____,
Land of the_____pride,
From every_____side
Let_____ring!

My_____country, thee,
Land of the noble_____,
Thy_____I love:
I_____thy rocks and_____,
Thy woods and_____hills;
My_____with rapture_____
Like that_____.

Let music swell the_____,
And_____from all the trees
Sweet freedom's_____:
Let mortal_____awake;
Let all that breathe_____;
Let rocks their silence break,
The_____prolong.

Our fathers' God, to Thee,
_____of liberty,
To Thee we sing:
_____may our land be_____
With freedom's_____light;
Protect us by Thy_____,
_____God, our King!

Samuel F. Smith

MY COUNTRY, 'TIS OF THEE

```
F C A D N I L R O H T U A I B
R M O T E Z E E R B G D H S R
E H O U I N M K W N H E M I I
E E N U N A I H O L Y I R N G
D E A D N T T L H A R D T G H
O K R I D T R S W G E E T S T
M S L L I R A Y L O R I N G R
P A R T A K E I Y O H E A R T
T H G I M F P O N E L D A W D
T H R I L L S A H E V N J T E
F L I B E R T Y D E S O H U L
C R S E W I A N S D H E B E P
R R E E V A U M N O E N G A M
A M E E N O H A L B E R T O E
M G N O S W L H S E U G N O T
```

ABOVE	MIGHT
AUTHOR	MOUNTAIN
BREEZE	NAME
BRIGHT	NATIVE
COUNTRY	PARTAKE
DIED	PILGRIM'S
FREE	RILLS
FREEDOM	RING
GREAT	SING
HEART	SONG
HOLY	SOUND
LAND	TEMPLED
LIBERTY	THEE
LONG	THRILLS
LOVE	TONGUES

MY JESUS, I LOVE THEE

My Jesus, I love_____, I know Thou art
_____;
For Thee all the_____of sin I resign;
My gracious_____, my Saviour art Thou;
If ever I loved Thee, my_____, 'tis now.

I love Thee_____Thou hast first loved me,
And_____my pardon on_____tree;
I love Thee for_____the thorns on Thy brow;
If ever I_____Thee, my Jesus, 'tis now.

I'll love Thee in life, I will love Thee in_____,
And_____Thee as long as Thou_____me breath;
And say when the_____lies cold on my
_____,
If ever I loved Thee, my Jesus, 'tis now.

In_____of glory and_____delight,
I'll ever adore Thee in heaven so_____;
I'll sing with the_____crown on my brow,
If_____I loved Thee, my Jesus, 'tis now.

William R. Featherstone

MY JESUS, I LOVE THEE

```
A W H A D E S A H C R U P K V
E L E N D E S T C X G H M E B
R E T S S S E L D N E A I Y E
W E B H V S F T I D D V N R C
J J C A L V A R Y S M J E O A
U E R U E F E L O V E D Y R U
Q S G A L T L I T T S T C M S
R U A D T H E H D N H U O A E
E S K I E P G J E E T L S N U
M V L O A I S Z E Z A T Y S S
E G N I R A E W E M E S J I E
E Z N B U D E A T H D E W O S
D S S P R A I S E A W I H N V
E V B S F O L L I E S M S S E
R N P O C R W D G L E X A D Z
```

BECAUSE
BRIGHT
BROW
CALVARY'S
DEATH
DEATHDEW
ENDLESS
EVER
FOLLIES
GLITTERING

JESUS
LENDEST
LOVED
MANSIONS
MINE
PRAISE
PURCHASED
REDEEMER
THEE
WEARING

O LITTLE TOWN OF BETHELEHEM

O little town of_____,
How_____ we see thee lie!
Above thy deep and_____ sleep
The_____ stars go by.
Yet in thy dark_____ shineth
The_____ Light;
The hopes and_____ of all the years
Are met in thee_____.

For Christ is born of_____,
And_____ all above,
While mortals sleep, the_____ keep
Their watch of_____ love.
O_____ stars, together
_____ the holy birth,
And_____ sing to God the_____,
And peace to men on earth.

How_____, how silently
The wondrous gift is_____!
So God_____ to human hearts
The blessings of His_____.
No ear may hear His coming,
But in this_____ of sin,
Where meek souls will _____ Him still,
The dear_____ enters in.

O holy_____ of Bethlehem!
_____ to us, we pray;
Cast out our sin, and enter in;
Be_____ in us today.
We hear the_____ angels
The great glad_____ tell;
O come to us, _____ with us,
Our Lord_____!

Phillips Brooks

O LITTLE TOWN OF BETHLEHEM

```
B S R M A R Y L T N E L I S G
E N S A M T S I R H C R E T A
T V T I E S R M S G N I D I T
H O E N U S A P O B W C I L H
L E N R E N E A E R O O M L E
E U A I L L F R C N N R R S R
H D S V G A I T A G D I N L E
E T N E E H S S M I E A N E D
M H E E B N T T R V R E S G C
M I A L C O R P I E I V E N H
A B I D E S E I C N N I S A A
N L T E K O E E H I G E I A N
U C H R I S T D I R H C A S N
E J Y B N S S E L M A E R D A
L I S O G L M E D E T R P E H
```

ABIDE	IMPARTS
ANGELS	KING
BETHLEHEM	MARY
BORN	MORNING
CHILD	PRAISES
CHRIST	PROCLAIM
CHRISTMAS	RECEIVE
DESCEND	SILENT
DREAMLESS	SILENTLY
EMMANUEL	STILL
EVERLASTING	STREETS
FEARS	TIDINGS
GATHERED	TONIGHT
GIVEN	WONDERING
HEAVEN	WORLD

O WORSHIP THE KING

O_____the King, all_____above,
And_____sing His power and His_____;
Our Shield and_____, the Ancient of Days,
_____in splendor, and_____with praise.

O tell of His might, O_____of His_____,
Whose robe is the light, whose_____space.
His_____of wrath the deep_____form,
And dark is His_____on the wings of the

_____.

Thy_____care what_____can recite?
It_____in the air, it shines in the_____.
It_____from the hills, it descends to the

_____,
And sweetly_____in the dew and the rain.

Frail_____of dust, and_____
  as_____,
In Thee do we_____, nor find_____to fail;
Thy_____how tender! how_____to the
  end!
Our_____, Defender, _____and Friend.

Robert Grant

REJOICE, YE PURE IN HEART

```
R E J O I C E R S S O R C H D
M A R Y E R U T P A R S E Y A
B Q S T R A I N S L T A A O R
P L S T I L L U H V R W N U K
B B I W A D E E T C K G T N
D A L S I N O J I N H S E H E
A I N O S L D T W I T G L U S
W O T N E I L A M R I F I O S
N N H I E M R I R V N G C N R
S A N D E R D M E D F N E L S
W A V E I T H A N K S D B L I
X E L O C H R I S T L Z C L N
E Q R U D Y T H R O U G H A G
A S S E N D A L G I E R U P V
C H A N T I N G B L A T S E F
```

ALL	HEART
AND	NIGHT
ANGEL	PURE
BANNER	RAPTURE
BLISS	REJOICE
CHANTING	SING
CHRIST	STANDARD
CROSS	STILL
DARKNESS	STRAINS
DAWNS	THANKS
FESTAL	THROUGH
FIRM	WARRIORS
GIVE	WAVE
GLADNESS	WITH
GOLDEN	YOUTH

ROCK OF AGES, CLEFT FOR ME

Rock of _____, cleft for me,
Let me hide _____ in Thee;
Let the _____ and the blood,
From Thy riven side which _____,
Be of sin the _____ cure,
_____ me from its guilt and _____.

Not the _____ of my hands
Can _____ Thy law's _____;
Could my _____ no respite know,
Could my tears _____ flow,
All for sin could not _____;
_____ must _____, and Thou alone.

_____ in my hand I _____,
Simply to Thy _____ I cling;
_____, come to Thee for dress,
Helpless, look to Thee for _____;
Foul, I to the _____ fly;
Wash me, _____, or I _____!

While I draw this _____ breath,
When mine eyes shall close in _____,
_____ I soar to worlds unknown,
See Thee on Thy _____ throne,
_____ of Ages, _____ for me,
Let me _____ myself in Thee.

Augustus M. Toplady

ROCK OF AGES, CLEFT FOR ME

```
C E S D N A M E D E A T H G F
H T R E B O R S F E N O T A O
F O U N T A I N R E W O P I R
J D K O R J A R L O M O N O E
M Y S E L F U P B Q B R L S V
I L E N R O C D S E G A T F E
U Y E D I H D U G V Z A L W R
S X E V Z E A L I M O E E I D
E U A B K W A T E R E V A S O
C S I A C L E F T T L N L I U
A S N H O E L P I U O H T I B
R N G A R M E N O T H I N G L
G T W H E N G C R O S S O D E
F U L F I L L A Y B M E O L B
Y T I G O P C B R I N G L T N
```

AGES
ATONE
BRING
CLEANSE
CLEFT
CROSS
DEATH
DEMANDS
DIE
DOUBLE
FLEETING
FLOWED
FOREVER
FOUNTAIN
FULFILL

GRACE
HIDE
JUDGMENT
LABORS
MYSELF
NAKED
NOTHING
POWER
ROCK
SAVE
SAVIOUR
THOU
WATER
WHEN
ZEAL

SAVIOUR, LIKE A SHEPHERD LEAD US

_____, like a_____lead us,
_____we need Thy_____care;
In Thy_____pastures feed us,
For our use Thy folds_____:
_____Jesus, Blessed Jesus,
Thou hast_____us, Thine we are.

We are_____; do Thou befriend us,
Be the_____of our way;
Keep Thy flock, from sin_____us,
_____us when we go astray:
Blessed Jesus, Blessed_____,
Hear, O_____us when we_____.

_____hast_____to receive us,
Poor and_____though we be;
Thou has mercy to_____us,
Grace to_____and power to_____:
Blessed Jesus, Blessed Jesus,
_____let us_____to Thee.

Early_____us seek Thy_____:
Early let us do Thy_____;
Blessed_____and only Saviour,
With Thy love our_____fill:
Blessed Jesus, Blessed Jesus,
Thou_____loved us, love_____still.

Dorothy A. Thrupp

SAVIOUR, LIKE A SHEPHERD LEAD US

```
D B L E S S E D I Y Q D A Y P
L N Y N O U O H T E A M L C R
G U A R D I A N A C E R B L E
Z R F B O U G H T X A U P E P
M A M N E B L N H E B U S A A
T E L L I O A E I M N R R N R
D W O S B S E M N E R D F S E
E T G C A O P R E N E S E E K
F R E E L F A V O R I W U R S
E B L L L O H D R O L I E E S
N P R O M I S E D T M L J W M
D I R U O I V A S L I L L H O
S H E P H E R D I E A I U A S
M K N R U T D I V J E S U S O
H E A R R K V E M U C H B T B
```

BLESSED
BOSOMS
BOUGHT
CLEANSE
DEFEND
EARLY
FAVOR
FREE
GUARDIAN
HAST
HEAR
JESUS
LET
LORD
MUCH

PLEASANT
PRAY
PREPARE
PROMISED
RELIEVE
SAVIOUR
SEEK
SHEPHERD
SINFUL
TENDER
THINE
THOU
TURN
US
WILL

SILENT NIGHT! HOLY NIGHT!

_____night! Holy_____!
_____is_____, all_____bright
'Round yon_____mother and_____!
Holy_____so_____and mild,
Sleep in_____peace.

Silent night! Holy night!
_____quake_____the_____!
Glories_____from heaven_____,
Heavenly_____sing: "_____!
Christ the_____is_____!"

Silent night!_____night!
_____of_____, love's_____ light
_____beams from Thy holy_____
With_____dawn of_____grace,
_____, Lord, at_____ _____!

Joseph Mohr

SILENT NIGHT! HOLY NIGHT!

```
N S H E P H E R D S R A Z I M
O B O U M V S K P A O F N L L
S K R Z S R T D F W T F A C E
P E T N A I D A R D A C S T J
R E D N E T P T S N Z S K J Q
S T S O H M T N T W D N R O B
B S J G N V F E R P S K J D I
Z Q I M D A L L E L U I A R R
T S J V L T S I A O S W A Z T
N K R O I V A S M D E J C N H
I O T P B V S D J M J Z H L F
G E D Q Y L N E V A E H I K J
R H O L Y N I G H T T D L V P
I T H Y O M J Z D K M O D L R
V D K R E D E E M I N G L T A
```

AFAR	JESUS
ALL	NIGHT
ALLELUIA	PURE
AT	RADIANT
BIRTH	REDEEMING
BORN	SAVIOR
CALM	SHEPHERDS
CHILD	SIGHT
FACE	SILENT
GOD	SON
HEAVENLY	STREAM
HOLY	TENDER
HOSTS	THE
INFANT	THY
IS	VIRGIN

STAND UP, STAND UP FOR JESUS

Stand up,_____up for Jesus,
Ye_____of the cross!
Lift_____His royal_____ —
It must not_____loss.
From victory unto_____
His_____shall He lead,
Till every foe is_____
And_____is Lord indeed.

Stand_____, stand up for Jesus,
The_____call obey;
Forth to the mighty_____
In this His_____day.
Ye that are_____, now serve_____
Against_____foes;
Let_____rise with danger,
And strength to strength_____.

Stand up, stand up_____Jesus,
Stand in His_____alone;
The arm of_____will fail you —
Ye dare not_____your own.
Put on the_____armor,
Each piece put on with_____;
Where_____calls, or danger,
Be never_____there.

Stand up, stand up for Jesus,
The_____will not be long;
This day the_____of battle,
The next, the victor's song.
To him that_____
A _____of life shall be;
He with the King of glory
Shall reign eternally.

George Duffield

STAND UP FOR JESUS

```
H N S T R E N G T H R D I T C
S E T R N L E H T E B E T E O
O E A U W H Y E J O Y R D P U
L E P S O G M E O L B E N M R
D I G T R O R E N N A B A U A
I G E N C R A B O O T M T R G
E H A R E G L O R I O U S T E
R M E Y S C H R I S T N W T C
S V A N Q U I S H E D N A A O
O R N H S D A T R K B U N L N
P E I G S U S R I G S C T N F
P M O I U M F I N T V A I Y L
O C A H S E L F T I O F N N I
S P R A E N F E E N O S G A C
E N L T V I C T O R Y O M U T
```

ARMY	OPPOSE
BANNER	OVERCOMETH
CHRIST	PRAYER
CONFLICT	SOLDIERS
COURAGE	STAND
CROWN	STRENGTH
DUTY	STRIFE
FLESH	SUFFER
FOR	TRUMPET
GLORIOUS	TRUST
GOSPEL	UNNUMBERED
HIGH	UP
HIM	VANQUISHED
MEN	VICTORY
NOISE	WANTING

SWEET HOUR OF PRAYER

Sweet_____of_____,
_____hour_____prayer,
That_____me from a_____of care,
And bids me at my_____ _____
Make all my wants and_____known!
In_____of_____and grief,
My soul has often found_____,
And oft_____the_____snare,
By thy return, sweet hour of prayer.

Sweet hour of prayer, sweet hour of prayer,
Thy wings shall my_____bear,
To Him whose truth and_____
_____the_____soul to bless;
And since He_____me seek His face,
_____His word and_____His grace,
I'll cast on Him my every care,
And_____for thee, sweet hour of prayer.

Sweet hour of prayer, sweet hour of prayer,
May I thy consolation share,
Till, from Mount Pisgah's_____height,
I view my_____and take my_____:
This robe of_____I'll drop, and rise
To seize the_____prize,
And shout, while passing_____the air,
Farewell, _____sweet hour of prayer!

William W. Walford

SWEET HOUR OF PRAYER

```
W P N I W A I T I N G D T B U
E S E A S O N S P E N G A G E
C V S T R E L I E F I E Y A F
A O E B I D S S E R T S I D A
F V H I J T R U S T S H L E T
S A S H L K I Q B E A X O P H
R G I G E E S O N R L U F A E
E A W U M C B L N D R L T C R
T Z M O E R U O H S E O Y S S
P E H R O F R C I R V M L E D
M T K H H T G T A U E F J L V
E N I T H R O N E L Q Y R I X
T H I A K E E P W E L O A Z P
F A R E W E L L O A W S D R C
F L I G H T Y E F L E S H B P
```

BELIEVE	LOFTY
BIDS	OF
CALLS	PRAYER
DISTRESS	PETITION
ENGAGE	RELIEF
ESCAPED	SEASONS
EVERLASTING	SWEET
FAITHFULNESS	TEMPTER'S
FAREWELL	THRONE
FATHER'S	THROUGH
FLESH	TRUST
FLIGHT	WAIT
HOME	WAITING
HOUR	WISHES
KEEP	WORLD

THE SOLID ROCK

My hope is built on nothing less
Than Jesus' blood and_____;
I dare not trust the sweetest frame,
But_____lean on Jesus' name.

When_____veils His lovely_____,
I rest on His_____grace;
In_____high and_____gale,
My anchor holds within the veil.

His oath, His_____, His blood
_____me in the whelming flood;
When all_____my soul gives way,
He then is all my hope and stay.

When He shall come with_____sound,
Oh, may I then in Him be_____;
_____in His righteousness alone,
_____to stand before the_____.

Refrain:

On Christ, the solid Rock, I stand;
_____other_____is sinking_____,
All_____ground is_____sand.

Edward Mote

THE SOLID ROCK

```
P M A K Y N M A I L L I W C S
A S U P P O R T M Y R A M O A
T G N I D N U O F U L Z A V R
R I G H T E O U S N E S S E T
U G G N I K N I S C M R A N S
M A R O U N D E E H M Y C A N
P A M E K R A H N A U R S N O
E W H O L L Y H K N R R S T O
T W S W D N U O R G B A E O B
D R E S S E D E A I E H L L A
A O T H E R H T D N A S T T M
T E S O V S A A B G U A L E L
E H T D E N O R H T N R U N E
M A T S R E N N A E J A A N H
F A C E Y M R O T S D H F A T
```

ALL
AROUND
COVENANT
DARKNESS
DRESSED
EVERY
FACE
FAULTLESS
FOUND
GROUND

OTHER
RIGHTEOUSNESS
SAND
SINKING
STORMY
SUPPORT
THRONE
TRUMPET
UNCHANGING
WHOLLY

TRUST AND OBEY

When we_____with the Lord
In the light of His_____,
What a_____He sheds on our_____!
While we do His good_____
He_____with us still,
And_____all who will trust and obey.

Chorus:

_____and obey, for there's no_____way
To be_____in_____,
But to trust and obey.

Not a_____can rise,
Not a cloud in the_____,
But His smile_____drives it_____;
Not a_____nor a fear,
Not a sigh nor a_____,
Can abide while we trust and obey.

But we never can_____
The_____of His_____
Until all on the_____we lay;
For the_____He shows,
And the joy He_____
Are for_____who will trust and_____.

Then in_____sweet
We will sit at His_____,
Or we'll walk by His_____in the way:
What He says we will do,
Where He_____we will go —
_____fear, only trust and obey.

J. H. Sammis

TRUST AND OBEY

```
D T E A R E A C C S E D I B A
T H E M X B W I T H W E S Z N
R S D N E S I H X T L Y I Y E
U T Y R O L G U Y A H V D E V
S L A S Z I E A R F A Z E B E
T F E L L O W S H I P S Z O R
L S A E R A O G A N P B P K I
L R D X Q U I C K L Y E S C T
I H P R O V E C B I D S J B N
W S Q A O U L S A T G T U E A
S H A D O W J R E H T O V I S
U E D L S M T E R I D W W N E
B S V K T E F T S N A S A G I
P A R O V A F B I U F L Y S K
W A L K L Y R U E L S O S N S
```

- ABIDES
- ALTAR
- AWAY
- BESTOWS
- DELIGHTS
- DOUBT
- FAVOR
- FEET
- FELLOWSHIP
- GLORY
- HAPPY
- JESUS
- LOVE
- NEVER
- OBEY
- OTHER
- PROVE
- QUICKLY
- SENDS
- SHADOW
- SIDE
- SKIES
- TEAR
- THEM
- TRUST
- WALK
- WAY
- WILL
- WITH
- WORD

WHAT A FRIEND

What a_____we have in_____,
All our_____and_____to bear!
What a_____to carry
_____to God in_____!
O what peace we often_____,
O what_____pain we bear,
All_____we do not_____
Everything to God in prayer.

Have we trials and_____?
Is there_____anywhere?
We should never be_____,
_____it to the_____in prayer.
Can we find a friend so_____
Who will all our_____share?
Jesus_____our_____weakness;
Take it to the Lord in prayer.

Are we_____and heavy_____,
_____with a load of care?
_____Savior, still our_____ —
Take it to the Lord in prayer.
Do thy friends_____, forsake thee?
Take it to the Lord in prayer;
In His_____He'll take and_____thee;
Thou_____find a_____there.

Joseph Scriven

WHAT A FRIEND!

```
S K J D O N N L U F H T I A F
F R I E N D J G O M T L E K O
E D I S C O U R A G E D L M R
I K L P C A R R Y V M H I S F
R N A I P I T G E H P Q M F E
G O D S I R A R Z R T R G D I
O W E E O R Y D I C A E K A T
R S N U E T E V F S T L O R D
U E B Y H R I T S H I E L D S
D L A I E L E C A L O S X W R
E R N B E C A U S E N Y O E E
P G M G U A C S N I S R W A F
V U E G S U S E J B R I E K U
C N E E D L E S S O L W B A G
P R E C I O U S S T Y R E V E
```

ARMS	LORD
BECAUSE	NEEDLESS
CARRY	PRAYER
CUMBERED	PRECIOUS
DESPISE	PRIVILEGE
DISCOURAGED	REFUGE
EVERY	SHIELD
EVERYTHING	SINS
FAITHFUL	SOLACE
FORFEIT	SORROWS
FRIEND	TAKE
GRIEFS	TEMPTATIONS
JESUS	TROUBLE
KNOWS	WEAK
LADEN	WILT

WHEN I SURVEY THE WONDROUS CROSS

When I survey the_____cross
On which the Prince of glory_____,
My_____gain I count but_____,
And pour_____on all my pride.

_____it, Lord, that I should_____,
Save in the_____of Christ, my God;
All the_____things that_____me most,
I_____them to His blood.

See, from His head, His_____, His feet,
Sorrow and love flow_____down;
Did e'er such love and_____meet,
Or thorns_____so rich a crown?

Were the_____realm of_____mine,
That were a_____far too small;
Love so_____, so divine,
_____my soul, my life, my all.

Issac Watts

WHEN I SURVEY THE WONDROUS CROSS

```
M J W O R R O S B Y E L S T O
K A M A Z I N G O I E U T H V
N O I W T U A E A H O S E D R
O W N F V E L O S S I N M E T
R O G T H A E A T C H A R M E
O N L F E H I L O O E T L A C
L D E D L I S N E M O W F N I
S R D I I N T I R P H E T D F
S O I G N E M G R O Y A S S I
F U C I M O D U L S S R E D R
O S E P E M E E D E A T H R C
R T T T R A O I A S Y A C M A
B H I O R E R U T A N V I U S
I F P R E S E N T D E V R E R
D U L V D H M J S Y E T E O I
```

AMAZING
BOAST
CHARM
COMPOSE
CONTEMPT
DEATH
DEMANDS
DIED
FORBID
HANDS

LOSS
MINGLED
NATURE
PRESENT
RICHEST
SACRIFICE
SORROW
VAIN
WHOLE
WONDROUS

WHEN THE ROLL IS CALLED UP YONDER

When the_____of the Lord shall_____,
    and time shall be no more,
And the_____breaks, _____, bright
    and_____;
When the_____of earth shall_____over
    on the other_____,
And the roll is called up yonder, I'll be there.

Chorus:
When the_____.........is called up yon---der,
When the roll........is_____up yon---der,
When the roll........is called up_____,
_____the roll is called up yonder, I'll be

_____.

On_____bright and_____morning when
    the_____in Christ shall_____,
And the_____of His_____share;
When the_____ones shall gather to their
    home_____the_____,
And the roll is called up yonder, I'll be there.

Let us_____for the Master from the dawn till
    _____sun,
Let us_____of all His_____love and
_____;
Then when all of life is_____, and our
_____on earth is_____,
And the roll is called up yonder, I'll be there.

James M. Black

WHEN THE ROLL IS CALLED UP YONDER

```
U L T E T E R N A L H A T H M
C L O U D L E S S D A H F R O
I T S C H O S E N Y A O T U R
E W O R K M U E M T A E L B N
K V O F A I R E D O P N D T I
O L L T H E R E F M E O L B N
L O A D H Y E O U R O B A L G
E L M T A S C R G D E V A S N
E C A R E R T E S H O R E K I
D G H T Y D I D Y O N D E R D
N M L E N L O O E T A K I W E
U S A O W O N D R O U S N H L
O G Y K R I D R O T E R I E L
S E I K S Y A T H N E E R N A
B E Y H M G N I T T E S N I C
```

BEYOND	RISE
CALLED	ROLL
CARE	SAVED
CHOSEN	SETTING
CLOUDLESS	SHORE
DEAD	SKIES
DONE	SOUND
ETERNAL	TALK
FAIR	THAT
GATHER	THERE
GLORY	TRUMPET
LABOR	WHEN
MORNING	WONDROUS
OVER	WORK
RESURRECTION	YONDER

WHILE SHEPHERDS WATCHED THEIR FLOCKS

While_____watched their_____by night,
All seated on the_____,
The_____of the Lord came down,
_____glory shone_____.

"_____not!" _____he, for
_____dread
Had seized their_____mind,
"Glad_____of great joy I bring
To you and all_____.

"To_____in David's town this_____
Is born of David's_____,
The_____who is Christ the_____,
And this_____be the sign:

"The_____Babe you_____shall find
To human view_____,
All_____wrapped in_____bands
And in a_____laid."

"All_____be to God on_____,
And to the_____be peace:
_____will_____from heaven to men
Begin and never_____."

Nahum Tate

WHILE SHEPHERDS WATCHED THEIR FLOCKS

```
A G N I H T A W S D B N A O C
T H E R E D P E T I D I N G S
R G M A N G E R H S E S G R N
O F O I R J A C F P I A E O M
U K L D R O L G E L M I L U E
B I S S R K U Q P A H D O N A
L T H E A V E N L Y S E J D N
E F E A R L Y X D E W E V U L
D Y P R L G L R Z D G L O R Y
M O H T U I O A M I G H T Y D
H U E H A I N O H E Q I A O U
G L R O V N A E D S M D L N K
I B D A M A N K I N D R I J D
H H S G S H T R O F E C N E H
F L O C K S A T B C U D E V F
```

AND	LINE
ANGEL	LORD
AROUND	MANGER
CEASE	MANKIND
DAY	MEANLY
DISPLAYED	MIGHTY
EARTH	SAID
FEAR	SAVIOR
FLOCKS	SHALL
GLORY	SHEPHERDS
GOOD	SWATHING
GROUND	THERE
HEAVENLY	TIDINGS
HENCEFORTH	TROUBLED
HIGH	YOU

ALL HAIL THE POWER OF JESUS' NAME

AMAZING GRACE

A MIGHTY FORTRESS IS OUR GOD

ALL HAIL THE POWER

All hail the power of Jesus' name!
Let angels prostrate fall;
Bring forth the royal diadem,
And crown Him Lord of all!

Ye chosen seed of Israel's race,
Ye ransomed from the fall,
Hail Him who saves you by His grace,
And crown Him Lord of all!

Let every kindred, every tribe,
On this terrestrial ball,
To Him all majesty ascribe,
And crown Him Lord of all!

O that with yonder sacred throng
We at His feet may fall!
We'll join the everlasting song,
And crown Him Lord of all!

Edward Perronet – John Rippon

AMAZING GRACE!

Amazing grace! how sweet the sound,
That saved a wretch like me!
I once was lost, but now am found,
Was blind, but now I see.

'Twas grace that taught my heart to fear,
And grace my fears relieved;
How precious did that grace appear
The hour I first believed!

Through many dangers, toils, and snares
I have already come;
'Tis grace hath brought me safe thus far,
And grace will lead me home.

When we've been there ten-thousand years,
Bright shining as the sun,
We've no less days to sing God's praise
Than when we first begun.

John Newton

A MIGHTY FORTRESS

A mighty fortress is our God,
A bulwark never failing;
Our helper He, amid the flood
Of mortal ills prevailing.
For still our ancient foe
Doth seek to work us woe;
His craft and power are great,
And, armed with cruel hate,
On earth is not his equal.

Did we in our own strength confide,
Our striving would be losing,
Were not the right Man on our side,
The Man of God's own choosing.
Dost ask who that may be?
Christ Jesus, it is He;
Lord Sabaoth His name,
From age to age the same,
And He must win the battle.

Martin Luther
Tr. by Frederick H. Hedge

BENEATH THE CROSS OF JESUS

BLESSED ASSURANCE

BRING THEM IN

BENEATH THE CROSS OF JESUS

Beneath the cross of Jesus
I fain would take my stand,
The shadow of a mighty Rock
Within a weary land;
A home within the wilderness,
A rest upon the way,
From the burning of the noontide heat
And the burden of the day.

Upon that cross of Jesus
Mine eye at times can see
The very dying form of One
Who suffered there for me;
And from my smitten heart with tears
Two wonders I confess —
The wonders of redeeming love
And my unworthiness.

I take, O cross, thy shadow
For my abiding place;
I ask no other sunshine than
The sunshine of His face;
Content to let the world go by,
To know no gain nor loss,
My sinful self my only shame,
My glory all the cross.

Elizabeth C. Clephane

BLESSED ASSURANCE

Blessed assurance, Jesus is mine!
Oh, what a foretaste of glory divine!
Heir of salvation, purchase of God,
Born of His Spirit, washed in His blood.

Chorus:

This is my story, this is my song,
Praising my Saviour all the day long;
This is my story, this is my song,
Praising my Saviour all the day long.

Perfect submission, perfect delight,
Visions of rapture now burst on my sight;
Angels descending bring from above
Echoes of mercy, whispers of love.

Perfect submission, all is at rest,
I in my Saviour am happy and blest;
Watching and waiting, looking above,
Filled with His goodness, lost in His love.

Fanny J. Crosby

BRING THEM IN

Hark! 'tis the Shepherd's voice I hear,
Out in the desert dark and drear,
Calling the sheep who've gone astray
Far from the Shepherd's fold away.

Chorus:

Bring them in, bring them in,
Bring them in from the fields of sin;
Bring them in, bring them in,
Bring the wandering ones to Jesus.

Who'll go and help this Shepherd kind,
Help Him the wandering ones to find?
Who'll bring the lost ones to the fold,
Where they'll be sheltered from the cold?

Out in the desert hear their cry,
Out on the mountains wild and high;
Hark! 'tis the Master speaks to thee,
"Go find my sheep wher-e'er they be."

Alexcenah Thomas

COME, THOU ALMIGHTY KING

COME, THOU FOUNT

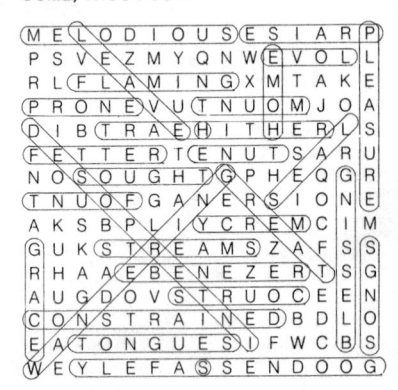

COUNT YOUR BLESSINGS

COME, THOU ALMIGHTY KING

Come, Thou Almighty King,
Help us Thy name to sing,
Help us to praise:
Father, all glorious,
O'er all victorious,
Come and reign over us,
Ancient of Days.

Come, Thou Incarnate Word,
Gird on Thy mighty sword,
Our prayer attend;
Come, and Thy people bless,
And give Thy word success:
Spirit of holiness,
On us descend.

Come, Holy Comforter,
Thy sacred witness bear
In this glad hour:
Thou who almighty art,
Now rule in every heart,
And ne'er from us depart,
Spirit of power.

To the great One in Three
Eternal praises be
Hence evermore;
His sovereign majesty
May we in glory see,
And to eternity
Love and adore.

Author Unknown

COME, THOU FOUNT

Come, Thou Fount of every blessing,
Tune my heart to sing Thy grace;
Streams of mercy, never ceasing,
Call for songs of loudest praise.
Teach me some melodious sonnet,
Sung by flaming tongues above;
Praise the mount — I'm fixed upon it —
Mount of Thy redeeming love.

Here I raise mine Ebenezer;
Hither by Thy help I'm come;
And I hope, by Thy good pleasure,
Safely to arrive at home.
Jesus sought me when a stranger,
Wandering from the fold of God;
He, to rescue me from danger,
Interposed His precious blood.

O to grace how great a debtor
Daily I'm constrained to be!
Let Thy goodness, like a fetter,
Bind my wandering heart to Thee:
Prone to wander, Lord, I feel it,
Prone to leave the God I love;
Here's my heart, O take and seal it;
Seal it for Thy courts above.

Robert Robinson – John Wyeth

COUNT YOUR BLESSINGS

When upon life's billows you are tempest tossed,
When you are discouraged, thinking all is lost,
Count your many blessings, name them one by one,
And it will surprise you what the Lord hath done.

Chorus:

Count your blessings,
Name them one by one;
Count your blessings,
See what God hath done;
Count your blessings,
Name them one by one;
Count your many blessings,
See what God hath done.

Are you ever burdened with a load of care?
Does the cross seem heavy you are called to bear?
Count your many blessings, every doubt will fly,
And you will be singing as the days go by.

When you look at others with their lands and gold,
Think that Christ has promised you His wealth untold;
Count your many blessings, money cannot buy
Your reward in heaven, nor your home on high.

So, amid the conflict, whether great or small,
Do not be discouraged, God is over all;
Count your many blessings, angels will attend,
Help and comfort give you to your journey's end.

Johnson Oatman, Jr.

DAY IS DYING IN THE WEST

DOES JESUS CARE?

FAITH OF OUR FATHERS

DAY IS DYING IN THE WEST

Day is dying in the west,
Heaven is touching earth with rest;
Wait and worship while the night
Sets her evening lamps alight
Through all the sky.

Lord of life, beneath the dome
Of the universe, Thy home,
Gather us, who seek Thy face
To the fold of Thy embrace,
For Thou art nigh.

When forever from our sight
Pass the stars, the day, the night,
Lord of angels, on our eyes
Let eternal morning rise,
And shadows end.

Refrain:

Holy, holy, holy, Lord God of Hosts!
Heaven and earth are full of Thee!
Heaven and earth are praising Thee,
O Lord most high!

Mary A. Lathbury

DOES JESUS CARE?

Does Jesus care when my heart is pained
Too deeply for mirth and song;
As the burdens press, and the cares distress,
And the way grows weary and long?

Chorus:

O yes, He cares — I know He cares,
His heart is touched with my grief;
When the days are weary, the long nights dreary,
I know my Saviour cares.

Does Jesus care when my way is dark
With a nameless dread and fear?
As the daylight fades into deep night shades,
Does He care enough to be near?

Does Jesus care when I've tried and failed
To resist some temptation strong;
When for my deep grief I find no relief,
Though my tears flow all the night long?

Does Jesus care when I've said good-by
To the dearest on earth to me,
And my sad heart aches till it nearly breaks —
Is it aught to Him? Does He see?

Frank E. Graeff

FAITH OF OUR FATHERS

Faith of our fathers! living still
In spite of dungeon, fire, and sword —
O how our hearts beat high with joy
When-e'er we hear that glorious word!
Faith of our fathers, holy faith!
We will be true to thee till death!

Our fathers, chained in prisons dark,
Were still in heart and conscience free;
How sweet would be their children's fate,
If they, like them, could die for thee!
Faith of our fathers, holy faith!
We will be true to thee till death!

Faith of our fathers! we will love
Both friend and foe in all our strife:
And preach thee, too, as love knows how,
By kindly words and virtuous life:
Faith of our fathers, holy faith!
We will be true to thee till death!

Frederick W. Faber

GOD BE WITH YOU

HARK! THE HERALD ANGELS SING

HOLY, HOLY, HOLY!

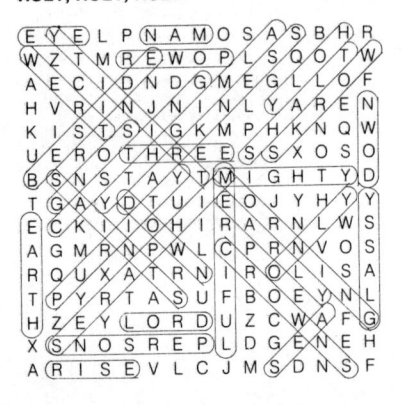

GOD BE WITH YOU

God be with you till we meet again;
By His counsels guide, up-hold you,
With His sheep securely fold you;
God be with you till we meet again.

God be with you till we meet again;
'Neath His wings protecting hide you,
Daily manna still provide you;
God be with you till we meet again.

God be with you till we meet again;
When life's perils thick confound you,
Put His arms unfailing round you;
God be with you till we meet again.

God be with you till we meet again;
Keep love's banner floating o'er you,
Smite death's threatening wave before you;
God be with you till we meet again.

Chorus:

Till we meet, till we meet,
Till we meet at Jesus' feet;
Till we meet, till we meet,
God be with you till we meet again.

Jeremiah E. Rankin

HARK! THE HERALD ANGELS SING

Hark! the herald angels sing,
"Glory to the newborn King:
Peace on earth, and mercy mild —
God and sinners reconciled!"
Joyful, all ye nations, rise,
Join the triumph of the skies;
With the angelic host proclaim,
"Christ is born in Bethlehem!"

Christ, by highest heaven adored,
Christ, the Everlasting Lord!
Late in time behold Him come,
Offspring of a Virgin's womb:
Veiled in flesh the Godhead see;
Hail the Incarnate Deity!
Pleased as man with men to dwell,
Jesus, our Emmanuel.

Hail the heaven-born Prince of Peace!
Hail the Sun of Righteousness!
Light and life to all He brings,
Risen with healing in His wings.
Mild He lays His glory by,
Born that man no more may die,
Born to raise the sons of earth,
Born to give them second birth.

Hark! the herald angels sing,
"Glory to the newborn King!"

Charles Wesley

HOLY, HOLY, HOLY!

Holy, Holy, Holy! Lord God Almighty!
Early in the morning our song shall rise to Thee;
Holy, Holy, Holy! Merciful and Mighty!
God in Three Persons, blessed Trinity!

Holy, Holy, Holy! All the saints adore Thee,
Casting down their golden crowns around the
    glassy sea;
Cherubim and seraphim falling down before Thee,
Which wert and art and evermore shalt be.

Holy, Holy, Holy! Tho' the darkness hide Thee,
Tho' the eye of sinful man Thy glory may not see,
Only Thou art holy; there is none beside Thee
Perfect in power, in love, and purity.

Holy, Holy, Holy! Lord God Almighty!
All Thy works shall praise Thy name, in earth,
    and sky, and sea;
Holy, Holy, Holy! Merciful and Mighty!
God in Three Persons, blessed Trinity!

Reginald Heber

I LOVE TO TELL THE STORY

I KNOW WHOM I HAVE BELIEVED

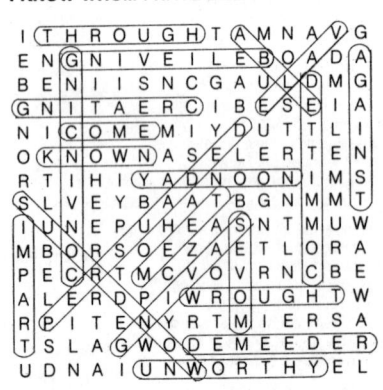

IN MY HEART THERE RINGS A MELODY

I KNOW WHOM I HAVE BELIEVED

I know not why God's wondrous grace
To me He hath made known,
Nor why, unworthy, Christ in love
Redeemed me for His own.

Chorus:

But "I know whom I have believed, and am
    persuaded that He is able
To keep that which I've committed
Unto Him against that day."

I know not how this saving faith
To me He did impart,
Nor how believing in His Word
Wrought peace within my heart.

I know not how the Spirit moves,
Convincing men of sin,
Revealing Jesus through the Word,
Creating faith in Him.

I know not when my Lord may come,
At night or noonday fair,
Nor if I'll walk the vale with Him,
Or meet Him in the air.

Daniel W. Whittle

I LOVE TO TELL THE STORY

I love to tell the story of unseen things above,
Of Jesus and His glory, of Jesus and His love.
I love to tell the story, because I know 'tis true;
It satisfies my longing as nothing else can do.

Chorus:

I love to tell the story,
'Twill be my theme in glory
To tell the old, old story
Of Jesus and His love.

I love to tell the story, more wonderful it seems
Than all the golden fancies of all our golden dreams.
I love to tell the story, it did so much for me;
And that is just the reason I tell it now to thee.

I love to tell the story, 'tis pleasant to repeat
What seems, each time I tell it, more wonderfully
    sweet.
I love to tell the story, for some have never heard
The message of salvation from God's own Holy
    Word.

I love to tell the story, for those who know it best
Seem hungering and thirsting to hear it like the rest.
And when, in scenes of glory, I sing the new, new
    song,
'Twill be the old, old story that I have loved so long.

Katherine Hankey

IN MY HEART THERE RINGS A MELODY

I have a song that Jesus gave me,
It was sent from heaven above;
There never was a sweeter melody,
'Tis a melody of love.

Chorus:

In my heart there rings a melody,
There rings a melody with heaven's harmony;
In my heart there rings a melody;
There rings a melody of love.

I love the Christ who died on Calvary,
For He washed my sins away;
He put within my heart a melody,
And I know it's there to stay.

'Twill be my endless theme in glory,
With the angels I will sing;
'Twill be a song with glorious harmony,
When the courts of heaven ring.

Elton M. Roth

I THINK WHEN I READ THAT SWEET STORY

IN THE GARDEN

JESUS, LOVER OF MY SOUL

I THINK WHEN I READ THAT SWEET STORY

I think when I read that sweet story of old,
When Jesus was here among men,
How He called little children as lambs to His fold,
I should like to have been with Him then.

I wish that His hands had been placed on my head,
That His arms had been thrown around me,
And that I might have seen His kind look when He said,
"Let the little ones come unto Me."

Yet still to His footstool in prayer I may go,
And ask for a share in His love;
And if I thus earnestly seek Him below,
I shall see Him and hear Him above.

Jemima Thompson Luke

IN THE GARDEN

I come to the garden alone,
While the dew is still on the roses,
And the voice I hear,
Falling on my ear,
The Son of God discloses.

Chorus:

And He walks with me, and He talks with me,
And He tells me I am His own,
And the joy we share as we tarry there,
None other has ever known.

He speaks, and the sound of His voice
Is so sweet the birds hush their singing,
And the melody
That He gave to me,
Within my heart is ringing.

I'd stay in the garden with Him
Though the night around me be falling,
But He bids me go;
Through the voice of woe,
His voice to me is calling.

C. Austin Miles

JESUS, LOVER OF MY SOUL

Jesus, Lover of my soul,
Let me to Thy bosom fly,
While the nearer waters roll,
While the tempest still is high.
Hide me, O my Saviour, hide,
Till the storm of life is past;
Safe into the haven guide,
O receive my soul at last!

Other refuge have I none;
Hangs my helpless soul on Thee;
Leave, ah, leave me not alone,
Still support and comfort me.
All my trust on Thee is stayed,
All my help from Thee I bring;
Cover my defenseless head
With the shadow of Thy wing.

Thou, O Christ, art all I want;
More than all in Thee I find;
Raise the fallen, cheer the faint,
Heal the sick, and lead the blind.
Just and holy is Thy name,
I am all unrighteousness;
False and full of sin I am,
Thou art full of truth and grace.

Plenteous grace with Thee is found,
Grace to cover all my sin;
Let the healing streams abound;
Make and keep me pure within.
Thou of life the Fountain art,
Freely let me take of Thee;
Spring Thou up within my heart,
Rise to all eternity.

Charles Wesley

JESUS LOVES ME

JESUS SAVES!

JOY TO THE WORLD!

JESUS SAVES!

We have heard the joyful sound:
Jesus saves! Jesus saves!
Spread the tidings all around:
Jesus saves! Jesus saves!
Bear the news to every land,
Climb the steeps and cross the waves;
Onward! — 'tis our Lord's command;
Jesus saves! Jesus saves!

Waft it on the rolling tide:
Jesus saves! Jesus saves!
Tell to sinners far and wide:
Jesus saves! Jesus saves!
Sing, ye islands of the sea;
Echo back, ye ocean caves;
Earth shall keep her jubilee:
Jesus saves! Jesus saves!

Sing above the battle strife,
Jesus saves! Jesus saves!
By His death and endless life,
Jesus saves! Jesus saves!
Sing it softly through the gloom,
When the heart for mercy craves;
Sing in triumph o'er the tomb —
Jesus saves! Jesus saves!

Give the winds a mighty voice,
Jesus saves! Jesus saves!
Let the nations now rejoice,
Jesus saves! Jesus saves!
Shout salvation full and free,
Highest hills and deepest caves;
This our song of victory —
Jesus saves! Jesus saves!

Priscilla J. Owens

JESUS LOVES ME

Jesus loves me! this I know,
For the Bible tells me so;
Little ones to Him belong;
They are weak, but He is strong.

Chorus:

Yes, Jesus loves me,
Yes, Jesus loves me,
Yes, Jesus loves me —
The Bible tells me so.

Jesus loves me! He who died,
Heaven's gate to open wide;
He will wash away my sin,
Let His little child come in.

Jesus loves me! loves me still,
Though I'm very weak and ill;
From His shining throne on high,
Comes to watch me where I lie.

Jesus loves me! He will stay
Close beside me all the way;
If I love Him, when I die
He will take me home on high.

Anna B. Warner

JOY TO THE WORLD!

Joy to the world! the Lord is come;
Let earth receive her King;
Let every heart prepare Him room,
And heaven and nature sing.

Joy to the earth! the Savior reigns;
Let men their songs employ;
While fields and floods, rocks, hills, and plains,
Repeat the sounding joy.

No more let sins and sorrows grow,
Nor thorns infest the ground;
He comes to make His blessings flow
Far as the curse is found.

He rules the world with truth and grace,
And makes the nations prove
The glories of His righteousness,
And wonders of His love.

Isaac Watts

MY JESUS, I LOVE THEE

MY COUNTRY, 'TIS OF THEE

O LITTLE TOWN OF BETHLEHEM

MY JESUS, I LOVE THEE

My Jesus, I love Thee, I know Thou art mine;
For Thee all the follies of sin I resign;
My gracious Redeemer, my Saviour art Thou;
If ever I loved Thee, my Jesus, 'tis now.

I love Thee because Thou hast first loved me,
And purchased my pardon on Calvary's tree;
I love Thee for wearing the thorns on Thy brow;
If ever I loved Thee, my Jesus, 'tis now.

I'll love Thee in life, I will love Thee in death,
And praise Thee as long as Thou lendest me breath;
And say when the deathdew lies cold on my brow,
If ever I loved Thee, my Jesus, 'tis now.

In mansions of glory and endless delight,
I'll ever adore Thee in heaven so bright;
I'll sing with the glittering crown on my brow,
If ever I loved Thee, my Jesus, 'tis now.

William R. Featherstone

MY COUNTRY, 'TIS OF THEE

My country, 'tis of thee,
Sweet land of liberty,
Of thee I sing:
Land where my fathers died,
Land of the pilgrim's pride,
From every mountain side
Let freedom ring!

My native country, thee,
Land of the noble free,
Thy name I love:
I love thy rocks and rills,
Thy woods and templed hills;
My heart with rapture thrills
Like that above.

Let music swell the breeze,
And ring from all the trees
Sweet freedom's song:
Let mortal tongues awake;
Let all that breathe partake;
Let rocks their silence break,
The sound prolong.

Our fathers' God, to Thee,
Author of liberty,
To Thee we sing:
Long may our land be bright
With freedom's holy light;
Protect us by Thy might,
Great God, our King!

Samuel F. Smith

O LITTLE TOWN OF BETHLEHEM

O little town of Bethlehem,
How still we see thee lie!
Above thy deep and dreamless sleep
The silent stars go by.
Yet in thy dark streets shineth
The everlasting Light;
The hopes and fears of all the years
Are met in thee tonight.

For Christ is born of Mary,
And gathered all above,
While mortals sleep, the angels keep
Their watch of wondering love.
O morning stars, together
Proclaim the holy birth,
And praises sing to God the King,
And peace to men on earth.

How silently, how silently,
The wondrous gift is given!
So God imparts to human hearts
The blessings of His heaven.
No ear may hear His coming,
But in this world of sin,
Where meek souls will receive Him still,
The dear Christ enters in.

O holy Child of Bethlehem!
Descend to us, we pray;
Cast out our sin, and enter in;
Be born in us today.
We hear the Christmas angels
The great glad tidings tell;
O come to us, abide with us,
Our Lord Emmanuel!

Phillips Brooks

O WORSHIP THE KING

REJOICE, YE PURE IN HEART

ROCK OF AGES, CLEFT FOR ME

O WORSHIP THE KING

O worship the King, all glorious above,
And gratefully sing His power and His love;
Our Shield and Defender, the Ancient of Days,
Pavilioned in splendor, and girded with praise.

O tell of His might, O sing of His grace,
Whose robe is the light, whose canopy space.
His chariots of wrath the deep thunderclouds
    form,
And dark is His path on the wings of the storm.

Thy bountiful care what tongue can recite?
It breathes in the air, it shines in the light,
It streams from the hills, it descends to the plain,
And sweetly distills in the dew and the rain.

Frail children of dust, and feeble as frail,
In Thee do we trust, nor find Thee to fail;
Thy mercies how tender! how firm to the end!
Our Maker, Defender, Redeemer and Friend.

Robert Grant

REJOICE, YE PURE IN HEART

Rejoice, ye pure in heart,
Rejoice, give thanks, and sing;
Your festal banner wave on high,
The cross of Christ your King.

With all the angel choirs,
With all the saints on earth,
Pour out the strains of joy and bliss,
True rapture, noblest mirth!

Yes, on through life's long path,
Still chanting as ye go;
From youth to age, by night and day,
In gladness and in woe.

Still lift your standard high,
Still march in firm array,
As warriors through the darkness toil
Till dawns the golden day.

Then on, ye pure in heart,
Rejoice, give thanks, and sing;
Your festal banner wave on high,
The cross of Christ your King.

Refrain:

Rejoice, rejoice,
Rejoice, give thanks, and sing!

Edward H. Plumptre

ROCK OF AGES, CLEFT FOR ME

Rock of Ages, cleft for me,
Let me hide myself in Thee;
Let the water and the blood,
From Thy riven side which flowed,
Be of sin the double cure,
Cleanse me from its guilt and power.

Not the labors of my hands
Can fulfill Thy law's demands;
Could my zeal no respite know,
Could my tears forever flow,
All for sin could not atone;
Thou must save, and Thou alone.

Nothing in my hand I bring,
Simply to Thy cross I cling;
Naked, come to Thee for dress,
Helpless, look to Thee for grace;
Foul, I to the fountain fly;
Wash me, Saviour, or I die!

While I draw this fleeting breath,
When mine eyes shall close in death,
When I soar to worlds unknown,
See Thee on Thy judgment throne,
Rock of Ages, cleft for me,
Let me hide myself in Thee.

Augustus M. Toplady

SAVIOUR, LIKE A SHEPHERD LEAD US

STAND UP FOR JESUS

SILENT NIGHT! HOLY NIGHT!

SAVIOUR, LIKE A SHEPHERD LEAD US

Saviour, like a shepherd lead us,
Much we need Thy tender care;
In Thy pleasant pastures feed us,
For our use Thy folds prepare:
Blessed Jesus, Blessed Jesus,
Thou has bought us, Thine we are.

We are Thine; do Thou befriend us.
Be the Guardian of our way;
Keep Thy flock, from sin defend us,
Seek us when we go astray:
Blessed Jesus, Blessed Jesus,
Hear, O hear us when we pray.

Thou hast promised to receive us,
Poor and sinful though we be;
Thou hast mercy to relieve us,
Grace to cleanse and power to free:
Blessed Jesus, Blessed Jesus,
Early let us turn to Thee.

Early let us seek Thy favor;
Early let us do Thy will;
Blessed Lord and only Saviour,
With Thy love our bosoms fill:
Blessed Jesus, Blessed Jesus,
Thou hast loved us, love us still.

Dorothy A. Thrupp

STAND UP, STAND UP FOR JESUS

Stand up, stand up for Jesus,
Ye soldiers of the cross,
Lift high His royal banner —
It must not suffer loss.
From victory unto victory
His army shall He lead,
Till every foe is vanquished
And Christ is Lord indeed.

Stand up, stand up for Jesus,
The trumpet call obey;
Forth to the mighty conflict
In this His glorious day.
Ye that are men, now serve Him
Against unnumbered foes;
Let courage rise with danger,
And strength to strength oppose.

Stand up, stand up for Jesus,
Stand in His strength alone;
The arm of flesh will fail you —
Ye dare not trust your own.
Put on the gospel armor,
Each piece put on with prayer;
Where duty calls, or danger,
Be never wanting there.

Stand up, stand up for Jesus,
The strife will not be long;
This day the noise of battle,
The next, the victor's song.
To him that overcometh
A crown of life shall be;
He with the King of glory
Shall reign eternally.

George Duffield

SILENT NIGHT! HOLY NIGHT!

Silent night! Holy night!
All is calm, all is bright
'Round yon virgin mother and child!
Holy infant so tender and mild,
Sleep in heavenly peace.

Silent night! Holy night!
Shepherds quake at the sight!
Glories stream from heaven afar,
Heavenly hosts sing: "Alleluia!
Christ the Savior is born!"

Silent night! Holy night!
Son of God, love's pure light
Radiant beams from Thy holy face
With the dawn of redeeming grace,
Jesus, Lord, at Thy birth!

Joseph Mohr

SWEET HOUR OF PRAYER

TRUST AND OBEY

THE SOLID ROCK

TRUST AND OBEY

When we walk with the Lord
In the light of His Word
What a glory He sheds on our way!
While we do His good will
He abides with us still,
And with all who will trust and obey.

Chorus:

Trust and obey, for there's no other way
To be happy in Jesus,
But to trust and obey.

Not a shadow can rise,
Not a cloud in the skies,
But His smile quickly drives it away;
Not a doubt nor a fear,
Not a sigh nor a tear,
Can abide while we trust and obey.

But we never can prove
The delights of His love
Until all on the altar we lay;
For the favor He shows,
And the joy He bestows
Are for them who will trust and obey.

Then in fellowship sweet
We will sit at His feet,
Or we'll walk by His side in the way;
What He says we will do,
Where He sends we will go —
Never fear, only trust and obey.

J. H. Sammis

SWEET HOUR OF PRAYER

Sweet hour of prayer, sweet hour of prayer,
That calls me from a world of care,
And bids me at my Father's throne
Make all my wants and wishes known!
In seasons of distress and grief,
My soul has often found relief,
And oft escaped the tempter's snare,
By thy return, sweet hour of prayer.

Sweet hour of prayer, sweet hour of prayer,
Thy wings shall my petition bear,
To Him whose truth and faithfulness
Engage the waiting soul to bless;
And since He bids me seek His face,
Believe His word and trust His grace,
I'll cast on Him my every care,
And wait for thee, sweet hour of prayer.

Sweet hour of prayer, sweet hour of prayer,
May I thy consolation share,
Till, from Mount Pisgah's lofty height,
I view my home and take my flight:
This robe of flesh I'll drop, and rise
To seize the everlasting prize,
And shout, while passing through the air,
Farewell, farewell, sweet hour of prayer!

William W. Walford

THE SOLID ROCK

My hope is built on nothing less
Than Jesus' blood and righteousness;
I dare not trust the sweetest frame,
But wholly lean on Jesus' name.

When darkness veils His lovely face,
I rest on His unchanging grace;
In every high and stormy gale,
My anchor holds within the veil.

His oath, His covenant, His blood
Support me in the whelming flood;
When all around my soul gives way,
He then is all my hope and stay.

When He shall come with trumpet sound,
Oh, may I then in Him be found;
Dressed in His righteousness alone,
Faultless to stand before the throne.

Refrain:

On Christ, the solid Rock, I stand;
All other ground is sinking sand,
All other ground is sinking sand.

Edward Mote

WHEN I SURVEY THE WONDROUS CROSS

WHAT A FRIEND!

WHEN THE ROLL IS CALLED UP YONDER

WHEN I SURVEY THE WONDROUS CROSS

When I survey the wondrous cross
On which the Prince of glory died,
My richest gain I count but loss,
And pour contempt on all my pride.

Forbid it, Lord, that I should boast,
Save in the death of Christ, my God;
All the vain things that charm me most,
I sacrifice them to His blood.

See, from His head, His hands, His feet,
Sorrow and love flow mingled down;
Did e'er such love and sorrow meet,
Or thorns compose so rich a crown?

Were the whole realm of nature mine,
That were a present far too small;
Love so amazing, so divine,
Demands my soul, my life, my all.

Issac Watts

WHAT A FRIEND

What a Friend we have in Jesus,
All our sins and griefs to bear!
What a privilege to carry
Everything to God in prayer!
O what peace we often forfeit,
O what needless pain we bear,
All because we do not carry
Everything to God in prayer.

Have we trials and temptations?
Is there trouble anywhere?
We should never be discouraged,
Take it to the Lord in prayer.
Can we find a friend so faithful
Who will all our sorrows share?
Jesus knows our every weakness,
Take it to the Lord in prayer.

Are we weak and heavy laden,
Cumbered with a load of care?
Precious Savior, still our refuge —
Take it to the Lord in prayer.
Do thy friends despise, forsake thee?
Take it to the Lord in prayer;
In His arms He'll take and shield thee;
Thou wilt find a solace there.

Joseph Scriven

WHEN THE ROLL IS CALLED UP YONDER

When the trumpet of the Lord shall sound, and time
   shall be no more,
And the morning breaks, eternal, bright and fair;
When the saved of earth shall gather over on the
   other shore,
And the roll is called up yonder, I'll be there.

Chorus:
When the roll. . . . . . . .is called up yon---der,
When the roll. . . . . . . .is called up yon---der,
When the roll. . . . . . . .is called up yonder,
When the roll is called up yonder, I'll be there.

On that bright and cloudless morning when the dead
   in Christ shall rise,
And the glory of His resurrection share;
When the chosen ones shall gather to their home
   beyond the skies,
And the roll is called up yonder, I'll be there.

Let us labor for the Master from the dawn till setting
   sun,
Let us talk of all His wondrous love and care;
Then when all of life is over, and our work on earth is
   done,
And the roll is called up yonder, I'll be there.

James M. Black

WHILE SHEPHERDS WATCHED THEIR FLOCKS

```
A G N I H T A W S D B N A O C
T H E R E D P E T I D I N G S
R G M A N G E R H S E S G R N
O F O I R J A C F P I A E O M
U K L D R O L G E L M I L U E
B I S S R K U Q P A H D O N A
L T H E A V E N L Y S E J D N
E F E A R L Y X D E W E V U L
D Y P R L G L R Z D G L O R Y
M O H T U I O A M I G H T Y D
H U E H A I N O H E Q I A O U
G L R O V N A E D S M D L N K
I B D A M A N K I N D R I J D
H H S G S H T R O F E C N E H
F L O C K S A T B C U D E V F
```

WHILE SHEPHERDS WATCHED THEIR FLOCKS

While shepherds watched their flocks by night,
All seated on the ground,
The angel of the Lord came down,
And glory shone around.

"Fear not!" said he; for mighty dread
Had seized their troubled mind,
"Glad tidings of great joy I bring
To you and all mankind.

"To you in David's town this day
Is born, of David's line,
The Savior who is Christ the Lord,
And this shall be the sign:

"The heavenly Babe you there shall find
To human view displayed,
All meanly wrapped in swathing bands
And in a manger laid."

"All glory be to God on high,
And to the earth be peace:
Good will henceforth from heaven to men
Begin and never cease."

Nahum Tate